DITTON PRIORS

A Settlement of the Brown Clee

Powkesmoor Steps — an old quarryman's route

DITTON PRIORS

A Settlement of the Brown Clee

by
Di Bryan

Logaston Press

LOGASTON PRESS
Little Logaston Woonton Almeley
Herefordshire HR3 6QH
logastonpress.co.uk

First published by Logaston Press 2006
Copyright © Di Bryan 2006

ISBN 1 904396 61 5
(978 1 904396 61 1)

Set in Garamond and Times New Roman by Logaston Press
and printed in Great Britain by
Biddles Ltd., King's Lynn

*Front cover illustration: Details of the 1768 estate map (se pp.xiv-xv) with (front)
pictures of the church, Howard Arms and Howard Arms Cottages and (rear)
Middleton Cottage, Home Farm and Middleton*

Contents

Acknowledgements

Eight years ago I was introduced to the hundreds, if not thousands, of documents relating to Ditton Priors and the Brown Clee in Shropshire Archives. Under the excellent tutorage of David Lloyd of Ludlow, the county archivist, Mary McKenzie and very helpful archivists, I learned the joys of searching for, deciphering and interpreting this material. In my desire to share this wealth of information, I was fortunate to find two Brown Clee soul mates, Chris Gadd and Caroline John, and before long, the Ditton Priors Local History Group was born. Further good fortune followed in that my husband Hugh found an interest in Victorian and later history allowing me to focus on medieval and earlier times that I find so rewarding. I was greatly aided in this early research by Brown Clee archaeology enthusiast Rona Cobb and Robin Cobb a geologist, whose knowledge of the complex geology of the hill came in very useful.

Two other local historians have provided material for interpretation and enthusiasm for the subject. John Hinton's published history of some of the parishes of Brown Clee was a wonderful eye-opener to the wealth of material I might be able to find about Ditton Priors and as John was an active member of my walking group I became a willing pupil as he pointed out many landscape features that less discerning eyes might miss. In a similar way, Bob Handley's wonderful collection of postcards, maps, books and artefacts were generously shared.

I soon learned that Ditton Priors never had a tithe map as its tithes were commuted before parliament required such surveys, but again fortune did not desert me as an estate map dated 1768 'turned up' within the village, having been saved from destruction by Christine Steele in the 1970s. The present owner, Dr Richard Groves, allowed full access and the map and its accompanying survey in Shropshire Archives, proved to be the key to medieval place-names, the open field system and much more besides. A generous grant from the Local Heritage Initiative allowed the map to be restored and displayed in the Brown Clee Health Centre and extended the area of research and the people involved. These extra researchers, Jane Kirk, Pam Gennard and Christine Mellings and I located documents relating to the parish of Ditton Priors all over the country and visits were made to the National Archives, the British Library, the Shakespeare Birthplace Trust, as well as the County Archives of Herefordshire, Warwickshire, Worcestershire, and Cumbria. Internet searches show more Ditton Priors documents in Essex and Berkshire, but these have been deemed not sufficiently important to make the journey. Officers of the Local History Group, particularly Martin Foley and Peter Gadd, have also been supportive and played a significant role in ensuring that this research was shared with a wider public in the two exhibitions staged by the group.

The LHI grant allowed us access to professionals such as Madge Moran, one of Shropshire's leading vernacular architectural historians. Through Madge we were able to record and dendrodate some of the houses found on the 1768 map. Many of the house recording group came from outside Ditton Priors and I am particularly grateful to Paul Walshe, Cecily Taylor, John Kirk, Mike Rayner, Paul Aston and local artists Kate Till and Gill Reilly for their sterling work that gave a deeper understanding to the development of post reformation Ditton Priors. Thanks are also due to the householders, the Shotton, Howells, Kirk, Mills-Keeling, Groves, Gadd and Warren families who allowed us unlimited access and made us welcome in their old homes. All the houses proved special although Wally Garbett's squatter cottage was described by Madge Moran as 'the jewel in our crown'. Sylvia and Bryan Colbatch of Hyde Farm deserve special thanks, not only did they share the long-hidden secrets of the oldest inhabited home in the parish with us, but Sylvia's collection of documents, maps and photographs proved invaluable in deciphering the history of the owners and occupants of Hyde Farm from Tudor times onwards.

The parishioners of Ditton Priors and members of the Local History Group have proved invaluable bringing us maps, photographs and artefacts relating to Ditton's history. Eileen Preece, born a Smallman, has contributed to our knowledge of this old Ditton family. We were very fortunate in Margaret Russell, who had the foresight to begin taking photographs of the village in the 1960s and so recorded many late twentieth-century changes. Gerald and Sylvia Hodnett were an unfailing source of local information and generously shared with us their newspaper articles and photographs of past times in Ditton Priors. It is not just local parishioners who have shared their past, many family historians come from all over Britain and the world to search for their Ditton Priors roots. To the Smallmans, Garbetts, Lewises, and above all the many Cartwrights and Morrises who come to browse our archives and leave us photographs, documents and information, I owe a debt of gratitude.

The farmers, without exception, have allowed me to wander over their land in search of old roads, boundary walls and other earthworks. Tom and Audrey Colbatch encouraged me to dig in their holloway to find the original cambered paved road with its regular kerbstones. Linda and Gerald Clarke allowed us to field walk in Middleton Priors where we found the Romano-British pottery and I was particularly grateful to the late Bill Lowe who walked with me over his land pointing out the remains of sluice gates belonging to the old water meadows as well as many other salient features. 'Walking the patch' has provided many hours of joy, finding geographical features such as valleys and springs whose names were bestowed in Saxon times and still survive to this day. Exploring the parish boundaries began several years ago with Vicki Bale and her dog Zulu but thanks to Bob Williams and his superior map reading abilities I have walked many more of the boundaries of the parish, often flailing through dense undergrowth to find the ditch and bank which was always discernible beneath later centuries of disturbance.

One of my greatest joys has been discussion with more rigorous researchers than myself such as David Poyner. Together with Hugh, it is David's knowledge of the industry on the hill that has guided my writing on this subject and on more than one occasion his information has resulted in the complete re-writing of various paragraphs. Hugh's knowledge of the industry of Ditton Priors has been greatly helped by information, documents and photographs from Michael Birt, a relative of Hamish Cross, and local farmer Brian Williams, whose interest in all things Brown Clee has been generously shared. Keith Beddoes, co-author of the definitive book on the Ditton Priors railway has also provided help and encouragement in this area.

Dr. Margaret Gelling, the English place-names expert has also been encouraging as I grappled with place-names to support my arguments about the history of pre-Conquest Brown Clee. Margaret's additions and amendments of my early drafts were both encouraging and exciting. Claire Mottershead's information about Neenton's frog meadow and well that belonged to the manor of Ditton in medieval times and production of the tithe map of Neenton allowed me to put the finishing touches to the hypothesis explored in the early chapters of the book, whilst the work of Ann Colburn on salting meat made it clear that the theory advanced made sense. For information on a later time, Michael Hodgetts, the archivist of Harvington Hall was generous with his time and research, sharing his work on Humphrey Pakington and the recusancy of Elizabethan times.

Friends, fellow researchers and other local historians, too numerous to mention have influenced me along the way, but I owe most to Dr. Sylvia Watts, who has been my Latin teacher, interpreter, mentor, editor and friend. Through Sylvia I attended the summer school at Keele University on medieval Latin and palaeography whose tutors included Dr. Charles Insley, a renowned Anglo-Saxon expert and Dr. Andy Fear, whose expertise in all things Roman is legendary. Both Charles and Andy were generous in giving guidance and encouragement as I developed my own theory of the history of Ditton during these periods. The Orderic Vitalis Medieval Latin group run by Sylvia has also been supportive in deciphering Ditton's manor court rolls, land charters and other Latin documents. I am particularly grateful to two members of this group, Peter Barton who tracked down the thirteenth-century deed on page 90 and Ralph Collingwood who found the deed on page 56 in the National Archives.

It is to the great misfortune of this work that Chris Gadd did not live to see the publication of the research that she helped to initiate and I hope that the book in some way is a tribute to her determination to make our ancestors live again through our studies. Chris's husband, Peter, continues to be a great supporter of the History Group and her daughter, Sarah Connor, has provided the drawings of how Ditton might have looked in past centuries so the family link continues. My final thanks must go to Hugh, who has been my researcher, map drawer, proofreader, family tree creator, archivist and general support, without him this book would not have happened.

Di Bryan
Ditton Priors
August 2006

Preface

In many ways this is a book of two halves, namely the period before the Battle of Hastings and the millennium afterwards. From the Norman Conquest onwards, I can draw on written records and other historians' work to interpret the general history of Brown Clee and that of Ditton Priors in particular. From the fourteenth century onwards the number of original documents that just relate to Ditton Priors is so numerous that I have been able to use only a small fraction of what is available. However, for the millennia before 1066 there are no written records of Ditton Priors and precious few for the Clee Hills. The landscape shows Iron Age hillforts and maybe Bronze Age structures, and books and research on pre-historic times covers these earthworks, not least because they are amongst the most impressive in Shropshire. But what happened on Brown Clee after the Roman invasion? Who owned the hill in the Romano-British period? How did the Anglo-Saxons make their presence felt? What was happening in Ditton Priors in the century before William the Conqueror arrived when the County of Shropshire was formed and England became a nation state? No historian that I know of has written or researched this period of Ditton Priors' existence and my attempt to piece together a cogent history of the six centuries before the Domesday Book of 1086 has been a real labour of love. For this reason the first few chapters are an academic foray into what I believe to be the most likely explanation for this period of Brown Clee's history.

With very little archaeological evidence, only Anglo-Saxon, or early and middle English place-names can give clues as to when and how the land was settled by English speakers and it is only by working backwards from information recorded in the Domesday Book that we can hypothesise about earlier times. Domesday tells us that Edwin Earl of Mercia owned Ditton Priors in 1066 and that the manor of Ditton, or Dodentone as it was then called, paid 2s. tax for the right to take salt from Droitwich. Only two other Shropshire manors possessed this salt right, so this indication that Ditton must have been rather special in pre-conquest times has fuelled my interest in deciphering the few clues that can be found to explain its importance. I hope readers will find my arguments as compelling as I do.

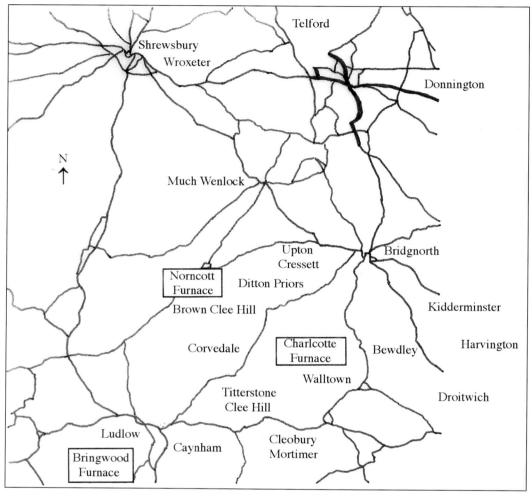

The south Shropshire places and furnaces relevant to the history of Ditton Priors

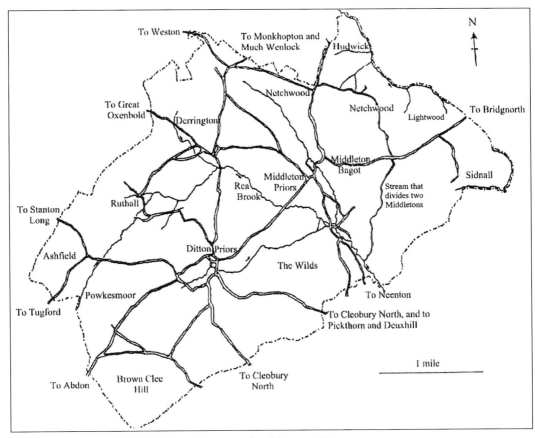

The Parish of Ditton Priors

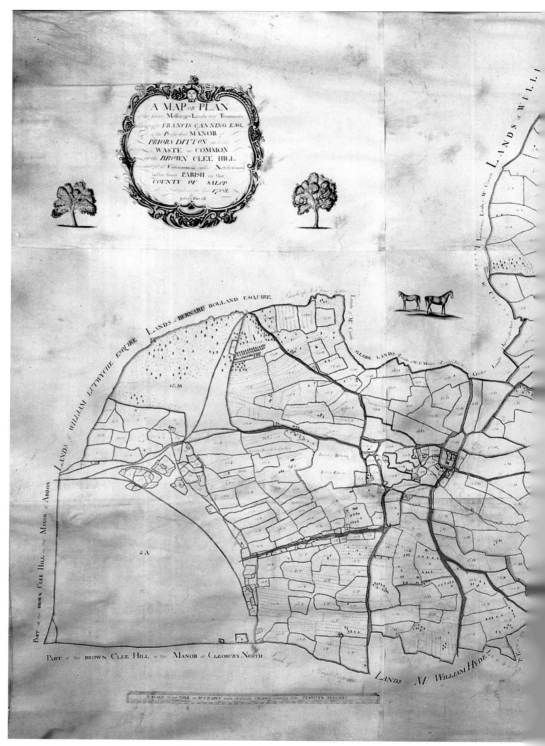

The 1768 estate map

With its accompanying survey, this was the key to the medieval history of Ditton Priors

CHAPTER 1
From Neolithic to Iron Age

The Clee Hills
The two tabletop masses of the Clee Hills form the eastern outcrop of the Welsh border hills and rise on a north-south axis from the Old Red Sandstone plateau. Their geological riches of coal, iron, dhustone and limestone, their plant resources of trees and grassland together with their surrounding fertile valleys, are central to the long history of the people of the Clee Hills. Titterstone Clee at 533 metres lies to the south with its associated settlements of Earls Ditton, Neen Savage and Cleobury Mortimer whilst at the northern end of the range, Brown Clee at 540 metres, rises over today's parishes of Stoke St Milborough, Clee St Margaret, Abdon, Ditton Priors, Cleobury North, Burwarton and Loughton. It is in this area that the history of Ditton Priors began because for thousands of years before the parish was named and its boundaries created, Brown Clee provided food, habitation, defence and burial sites for our ancestors.

Neolithic Hunters and Settlers
More than five thousand years ago, the area around Brown Clee, like most of Shropshire, was densely wooded. Alder and willow flourished in river valleys and other damp places whilst broadleaf trees, predominantly lime and oak, covered vast tracts of land.[1] Brown Clee, with its mineral wealth as yet unexploited, provided habitats for birds and animals as well as producing plants, fruits and nuts. Finds of ancient artefacts indicate that Neolithic people exploited this landscape maybe coming for game initially and later settling in the area. The tools found indicate the sort of activities that took place around the Brown Clee. Heavily weathered Neolithic tools found at Lightwood in 1970 are some of the earliest archaeological finds from Ditton Priors and were used for the processing of prey rather than hunting itself.[2] The finds consisted of four different types of scraper and a 'strike-a-light', namely an iron stained flint used for making fire. Similar tools were found on Brown Clee,[3] but the best-authenticated hunting tool is a leaf arrowhead found on Nordy Bank.[4] This is the first evidence for hunting on Brown Clee, an activity that recurs many times in the story of the hill and history of Ditton Priors. Late Neolithic finds indicate that a community was resident in the area of the Brown Clee. A well worn stone adze found at Earnstrey suggests woodworking activity[5] whilst two polished stone axes, one discovered in the grounds of Burwarton Hall in 1885[6] and the other in Abdon Burf quarry in 1936[7] reveal a structured and well organised Brown Clee population that had established trading links with other late Neolithic peoples. Such axes are well known and because of their polished and unused surfaces are assumed to be of ceremonial impor-

tance. These two axes were made and crafted in the Lake District, and exchanged or traded over a wide area.

The Bronze Age: *c.*2,500 BC – 700 BC

By 2,500 BC, metalworking, first in copper and later in bronze, was developing in some populous areas, but in this part of Britain, as elsewhere, the people continued to use stone tools well into the first millennia BC. Thousands of these Bronze Age stone tools, typically made from flint of the Marlborough Downs, have been found along the route of the pre-historic Clun-Clee Trackway, thought to date to the early Bronze Age, when the trade in stone axes was already dying out. The route, which in many places is ill defined, began in Wales and crossed the Severn at Bewdley having passed around Titterstone Clee Hill.[8] Brown Clee, situated close to this well-used trackway, must have witnessed a certain amount of human movement in and out of the area. Such interchange is likely to have brought new ideas and technology to the residents of Brown Clee, although no trace can be found of any of the bronze metal tools that give the name to the age.

During the Bronze Age the people dwelling on and around Brown Clee cleared some of the woodland, probably with tools such as the dhustone axe found at Oakwood in the early twentieth century[9] as they developed new farming techniques. Stamper (1989) notes that small fields, usually surrounded by banks or stone walls, grew grain crops such as emmer wheat and barley whilst the movement of herds to graze upland pastures in the summer must have had a significant impact on agricultural life around the Clee Hills. One can imagine that most permanent habitation as well as winter pastoral life was at the lower levels where today's modern villages are situated (see map p.*xii*), whilst summer quarters were established higher up Brown Clee. The landscape used to contain evidence of Bronze Age inhabitants of Brown Clee as at least one and possibly two burial cairns were recorded on the summit before being destroyed by twentieth century quarrying. The large cairn in the north-west section of the later Iron Age enclosure is likely to have been that of a chieftain. It was described as rising eight feet above the inner level of the later enclosure

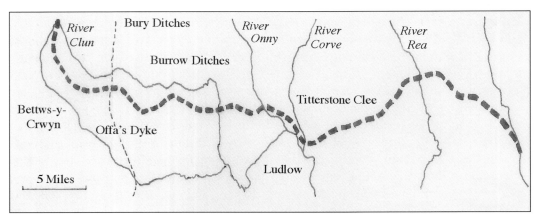

Clun-Clee prehistoric trackway, albeit indistinct in places, identified by Lilly Chitty. (Drawn by Hugh Bryan)

and large flat-sided blocks, well fitted together, were found inside the cairn.[10] No human remains were found during the excavation. Large hilltop cairns can still be seen on the Long Mynd and Stiperstones indicating widespread similarities between the Bronze Age people of what was to become South Shropshire.

It is probable that the Bronze Age people of the hill, with their agricultural lifestyle, widespread trading links, ceremonial practices and burial rites built a settlement or some form of enclosure on the summit of the hill which was utilised by later Iron Age people when they began to build the hilltop enclosure that is now called Abdon Burf.

The Iron Age to Roman Britain: 700 BC – 43 AD

In the millennia before the Romans invaded, large swathes of Britain, from north-west England to present day Sussex gradually became home to a large number of settlements subsequently termed hillforts. Indeed in this part of Shropshire it is difficult to find a hilltop that does not have some form of an Iron Age enclosure on its summit, evidence that supports the contention that the population of Iron Age Britain was quite substantial. The enclosure on Abdon Burf was recorded in the 1830s when Charles Hartshorne, the nineteenth-century antiquary visited the burf. His drawing shows an irregular oval measuring 403m by 202m and enclosing a space of 8 ha. The walls were described as being from 1m to 3m high and made of dhustone. A ridgeway connected the enclosure with the smaller hillfort to the south on Clee Burf. Both inside and outside the ramparts a number of circular hollows were recorded, some of which may have been later coal workings, but many are now recognised as Iron Age constructions for habitation, cattle holding or grain storage.[11] Inturned entrances with guard-rooms were also recorded, although no dating evidence was discovered.[12] Excavations of neighbouring hillforts, such as Caynham Camp and Titterstone

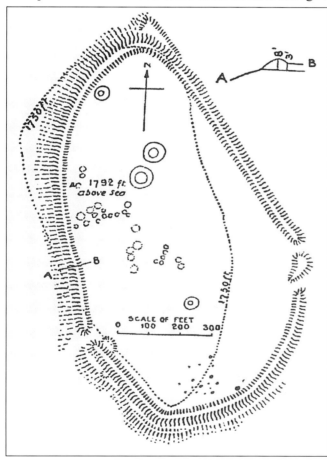

Abdon Burf hillfort surveyed in the 1930s from Hartshorne C., 1841, Salopia Antiqua *John Parker*

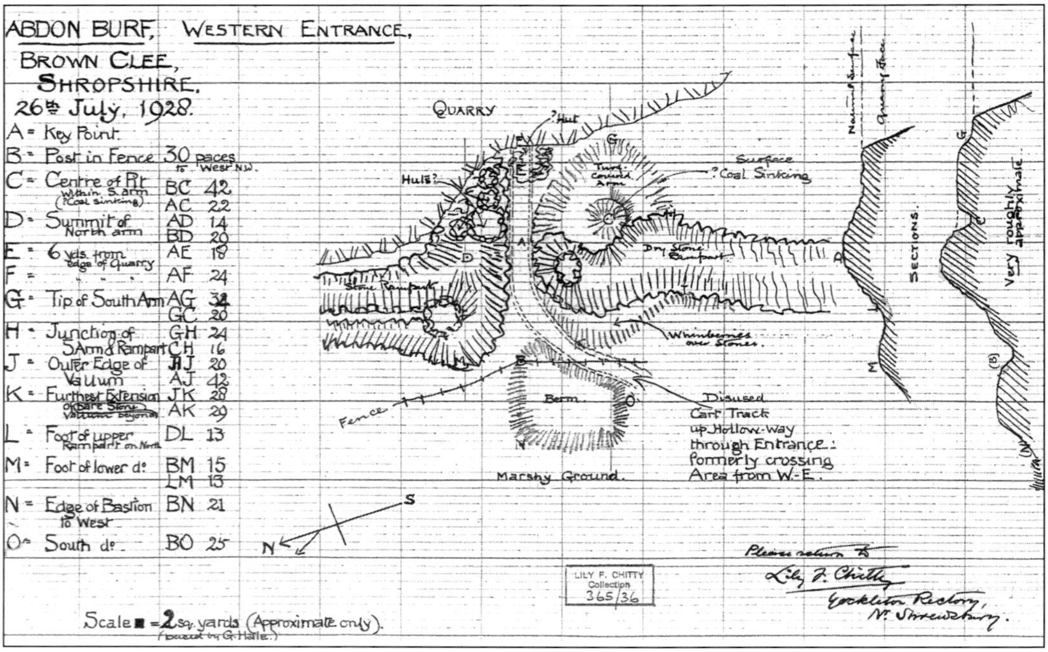
ABDON BURF, WESTERN ENTRANCE,
BROWN CLEE,
SHROPSHIRE.
26th July, 1928.
A = Key Point.
B = Post in Fence 30 paces to West NW.
C = Centre of Pit within S. arm (?Coal sinking) BC 42 AC 22
D = Summit of North arm AD 14 BD 20
E = 6 yds. from Edge of Quarry AE 18
F = " " " AF 24
G = Tip of South Arm AG 32 GC 20
H = Junction of S Arm & Rampart GH 24 CH 16
J = Outer Edge of Vallum HJ 20 AJ 42
K = Furthest Extension of Bare Stone JK 28 AK 29
L = Foot of upper Rampart on North DL 13
M = Foot of lower d° BM 15 LM 13
N = Edge of Bastion to West BN 21
O = South d° BO 25
Scale ■ = 2 sq. yards (Approximate only).
QUARRY
?Hut
Huts?
Turf-Covered Arm
Surface ?Coal Sinking
Dry Stone Rampart
Stone Rampart
Whinberries over Stones.
Fence
Berm.
Marshy Ground.
Disused Cart Track up Hollow-way through Entrance: formerly crossing Area from W.-E.
SECTIONS.
Very roughly approximate.
S
N
Please return to Lily F. Chitty Yockleton Rectory, Nr. Shrewsbury.
LILY F. CHITTY Collection 365/36

The western entrance of Abdon Burf hillfort drawn by Lily Chitty in 1928 when she spear-headed rescue archaeology before the hillfort was destroyed by quarrying (SA 365/36)

Clee, reveal just how complex the Abdon Burf enclosure could have been. Both Caynham and Titterstone were in use for nearly a thousand years, with modifications and rebuilding taking place throughout this period. In about 400 BC, Titterstone Clee gained inturned entrances that included guardrooms, and walls were raised and strengthened.[13] Finds from Caynham and the Iron Age settlement at Bromfield near Ludlow reveal local pottery that used crushed dhustone as a strengthening material. Stanford (1982) notes that a minor group of potters were active in the Clee Hills in the Iron Age supplying sites within a 20-kilometre radius of Titterstone Clee.[14]

Without evidence for large-scale immigration into the area, it seems probable that the people living around the Brown Clee in the Iron Age were descended from those of earlier times. Over thousands of years they had settled the area, cleared some of the woodland, especially the more fertile lower areas, and created an agricultural society prepared to defend its territory against either neighbours or enemies from further afield. In the centuries before the Roman Conquest in 43 AD, these people had become part of the tribe named the Cornovii whose headquarters were probably situated on the hilltop settlement of The Wrekin. However, in the Clee Hills, the Iron Age camp on Titterstone Clee was three times larger than any other camp in the vicinity. This may reflect both Titterstone's strategic importance and the prominence of the group of people and their chieftains who inhabited it, while the people of the Brown Clee hillforts were not as dominant as those of Titterstone. This lack of strategic importance for Brown Clee was to serve it well when the Romans finally reached these parts in the fifth decade of the first century.

CHAPTER 2
From Romano-British Cornovii to Mercian Holding

Romano-British Cornovii: 43 AD – 680s

The absence of a tribal coinage indicates that the Cornovii who inhabited an extensive area of western Britain were a loose federation of peoples.[15] It is impossible to know the extent of their territory before the Roman invasion as the province was only subsequently delineated for Roman administrative purposes. However as the Roman Cornovii canton stretched from north of modern day Chester to the River Wye in the south and from east of Droitwich to the Welsh foothills it is probable that it bore some relationship to an earlier territory.[16] Unlike some other British tribes, the Cornovii never had trading or other links with the Romans prior to the incorporation of Britain into the Roman empire so the local population probably viewed their arrival in this part of the world with some trepidation.

Although we know from excavations that several local hilltop settlements were subjected to attack at some time during their existence, there is no evidence that any of the Brown Clee hillforts of Abdon Burf, Clee Burf and Nordy Bank experienced sustained fighting between the Cornovii and the Romans. This may indicate that the tribe, or at least the Brown Clee people, accepted Roman rule with little or no resistance – a situation the Romans must have encouraged as various tribes continued to resist the invaders even after the great revolt spearheaded by Boudicca was crushed in 61 AD. Until 90 AD, the Cornovii were under military control directed principally from the legionary fort at Wroxeter that had been established before 75 AD.[17] During this early period an auxiliary fort was built at Walltown, near Neen Savage. This fort was later rebuilt and occupied until the end of the second century indicating the importance for the Romans to maintain a military presence in the area around the Titterstone Clee plateau.

Neither Roman settlement nor artefacts have been found in the immediate vicinity of Brown Clee, although finds have been reported from both Monkhopton and Upton Cressett. In the absence of any known Roman presence we can only speculate on the situation here using other examples of Roman occupation to guide our ideas. After the initial military rule, it seems possible that the leaders of the population living in or near the hillforts of Abdon Burf, Clee Burf and Nordy Bank could have been appointed by the Romans to be their chief administrators of the area.[18] If so, they would have been responsible for collecting the *tributum*, a mixture of money and goods demanded by the Romans, and sending it to a central point such as Wroxeter. As the Cornovii did not strike their own coins it is likely that our Brown Clee people sent grain, slaves and hunting dogs, all highly prized by the invaders. With the hunting ground of the Brown Clee at their disposal, it seems reasonable to suggest that our population would have bred dogs to hunt on the slopes of the hill. It is thought that the Romans found little, if any, reason for commercially exploiting the stone or ironstone of the Clee hills, although the people living here certainly used both, and may have sent iron nodules along with other goods to Wroxeter.

When the army left Wroxeter in about 90 AD it became a civilian settlement, known as the capital of the Cornovii.[19] As the fourth largest city in Roman Britain, it was a place of consequence with baths, a forum and – by the fourth century – is also likely to have had a Christian church.[20] It is the absence rather than the presence of Roman villas in the south Shropshire countryside that leads to the speculation that the well-endowed city of Wroxeter became the dwelling place of high-ranking Cornovii who received an income from rents and produce of their estates,[21] and it may be that our Brown Clee chieftains also sought a more comfortable existence in the town and left the running of the 'Brown Clee estate' to bailiffs. If this suggestion of absentee landlords is correct then it is a recurrent feature of Ditton's history.

Land of the Magonsaete: 410 – c.720

After the collapse of Roman administration in the early fifth century, life on and around the Brown Clee probably continued much as before with agriculture being the principal industry of the area, and although one sherd of locally produced Romano-British pottery, dated c.450 AD, has been found in the parish of Ditton Priors[22] it does not tell us much about the lives of the people living around Brown Clee.

In western Britain the tribal system re-emerged with British kings and princes ruling large territories and collecting the *tributum*, usually of food goods. By the early seventh century the might of the English or Anglo-Saxon peoples led by Penda, the first recorded king of Mercia had reached this area. The history of the Clee Hills and Brown Clee in particular is linked with the Mercian kings so it is worth examining their origins. 'Mercian' means the people of the border and it is thought they began their rise to power in the late fifth century in the area around the Trent River basin, with Tamworth, Repton and Lichfield being their principal settlements.[23] Gradually over a number of years they became the overlords of the many tribal chiefdoms and petty kingdoms of central and western England. They appear to have done this without resorting to outright warfare, although clearly they had both military strength and power to convince British tribes that it was worth aligning themselves with English Mercians. One of the sub-kingdoms that acknowledged Mercian overlordship in the later half of the seventh century was the Magonsaete and information regarding the foundation of the monastery at Much Wenlock can be used to construct a theory indicating that the Magonsaete royal family, founders of the monastery, also owned the land of the Clee Hills.

Small piece of Romano-British pottery found by fieldwalking in Middleton Priors in 2001. The ridges are the finger marks of the potter

England in the eighth and early ninth centuries when Lindsey and the lands of the Hwicce, Magonsaete and Wreocensaete were part of the greater kingdom of Mercia

Wenlock's founder, King Merewalh, ruled the Magonsaete, although it is not known for sure how he came to control the sub-kingdom.[24] Later medieval documents claim him to be a son of Penda, but Pretty (1989) makes a convincing argument for him to be of British rather than English stock.[25] His name probably meant 'famous Welshman' so it seems wise to have an open mind as to his origins.[26]

The principal seat of the Magonsaete was in present day north Herefordshire, although their territory included the Clee Hills and extended to the River Severn. This can be inferred from a mixture of myth, genuine Anglo-Saxon charters and twelfth-century writings that supposedly draw on much earlier documents. King Merewalh had two sons from his first marriage, Merchelm and Mildfrith, and then married Domina Eafe, a Christian princess of Kent.[27] This marriage produced three daughters, all of whom became saints of the early church. Mildgyth and Mildthryth lived their saintly lives elsewhere, but the youngest daughter, Mildburh, belongs to this part of Shropshire. Merewalh is deemed to have converted to Christianity and founded a monastery at Wenlock prior to 685, under the tutelage of Botulph's monastery of Iken in Suffolk. Mildburh, as its second abbess, ruled over this double monastery of both monks and nuns until her death in the late 720s. The lands given to Wenlock[28] for its support by Merewalh and his two sons indicate the extent of Magonsaete territory, but it is the lands given between 674 and 704 by Mildburh's half-brothers that indicate their ownership of the Brown Clee area.[29] This land is described as being around the Clee Hill and certainly included present day Stoke St. Milbourgh, some land in Chelmarsh and some by the River Corve, likely to have been Stanton Long.[30]

The extent of the Diocese of Hereford, established *c.*690, also confirms the bounds of Magonsaete territory. Hillaby writes that Merewalh's son, Mildfrith, '… collaborating with his half-sister, established a tribal diocese on Roman lines with its bishop's seat at Hereford.'[31] In general, the northern boundary of the diocese is the River Severn, just like the boundary of the land of the Magonsaete, but the fact that Madeley and Little Wenlock, possessions of Mildburh's monastery that lie north of the River Severn, are in Hereford diocese is proof enough of Mildburh's influence in this area.

Merewalh's Christianity shows that the religion was practised in this region during the seventh century as it probably had been since Roman times given the zeal of some of the early Welsh saints who operated in this area. Indeed, Gelling (1979) believes that there is enough place-name and archaeological evidence to support the theory that when the English arrived in these parts they retained their pagan beliefs for no more than a generation before becoming Christian. The priests based at the monastery (or minster) of

The crypt at Repton, the burial place of Mercian royalty, as drawn in c.1896

Wenlock administered Christianity in the wider neighbourhood, and it may be that they served Ditton Priors, although it is also possible that the minster at Morville or that at Stottesdon covered this area before parishes with their own churches were established.

Mildburh's brothers died in the 720s without heirs and the sub-kingdom of the Magonsaete was subsumed into the greater kingdom of Mercia, then ruled by King Aethelbald. Later evidence from Domesday Book, compiled in 1086, (see Chapters 4 and 5) suggests that the Brown Clee lands of the royal Magonsaete were directly transferred into the hands of Aethelbald of Mercia and his successors. At this time land holdings covered extensive areas, called great or multiple estates and place-name evidence suggests that the Brown Clee area was only part of one such estate that comprised the whole of the Clee Hill range.[32] Settlements scattered throughout this large area usually consisted of a single farm run by one or two families with delineated fields and boundaries. Such a pattern had existed since the Iron Age or earlier but in the early eighth century each would have had a British or maybe more recent Old English name.[33] Such is the importance of place-names in determining the history of Brown Clee that the subject will be dealt with in the following chapter.

Life Under Mercian Rule
A succession of strong and long-reigning kings, from Wulfhere in 656 to Coenwulf in 821 extended and consolidated Mercian rule to such an extent that this era was called the 'Mercian supremacy'. At times their territory covered most of England, including parts of Kent, Lincolnshire and London, but Repton remained one of their strongholds with many of the kings and princes of Mercia being buried in the monastery there. King Offa (757-796) and Charlemagne corresponded as monarchs of equal status and at one time they even considered marriage between their children. Silver pennies bearing Offa's likeness were minted indicating a thriving market economy. Offa's reign also saw a continuation of the Mercian construction of defensive settlements[34] including the large earthwork known today as Offa's Dyke.

The Brown Clee people of this Mercian age would have experienced living in a well-structured military society with agriculture at its heart, but they had a price to pay for the prosperity it brought. Place-name evidence suggests that the division of the big Clee estate into the smaller manors we know today seems likely to have taken place in the late eighth or early ninth century and each manor had a duty to provide what was called the three-fold obligation. This consisted of the provision of men to undertake labour services in three vital areas, namely for the building and repair of bridges, for the building and repair of fortifications and for the provision of a standing army. The people of the newly formed manors of the Clee Hills would have sent men, and their share of the *tributum*, to wherever their Mercian overlords directed. It seems likely that Offa kept direct control of the new manor that would become known as Ditton Priors and it may be that he directed his tenants to the Welsh border to build their share of his dyke.

Offa's son ruled for only a few months, but King Coenwulf, his successor, continued to rule a powerful Mercia until his death in 821. By this date internal and external factors were combining to ensure the decline of the Royal house of Mercia.

By the mid ninth century, a series of less powerful kings and increased Viking raids caused the large kingdom of Mercia to be split into two with the eastern half under Viking rule and known as the Danelaw. Mercian kings continued to rule the western half, but such were the difficulties that King Burgred abandoned his throne in 874 and was replaced by the Viking appointed ruler, Coelwulf, whom the Anglo-Saxon Chronicle called 'an unwise thane of the king'.[35] From now on, Mercian rulers are perceived as part of King Alfred of Wessex's campaign to drive out the Viking invaders and thus create a united kingdom of England.

CHAPTER 3
Place-Names, Boundaries and Agriculture of the Brown Clee

Pre-Conquest Place-Names

The peoples who lived in this part of Mercia did not use pottery so Anglo-Saxon archaeological finds are exceedingly rare. Similarly, Ditton Priors and most of the Clee Hills do not feature in pre-conquest written documents so place-names are the principal source for interpreting the local scene.

The place-names of the Brown Clee, with few exceptions, belong to the Middle English period (750-950 AD). However, two earlier place-names will be discussed first. The name **'Clee'** has exercised the minds of many philologists, but after much discussion, Dr Gelling writes, 'It seems to me most satisfactory to consider that the base of 'Clee' is an Old English name '*Cleo*' which means 'ball-shaped massif'.[36] If this supposition is correct, then it means that the name *'Clee'* probably dates to the time when the Mercian kings inherited the lands of the Magonsaete in the 720s or even earlier. The prefix 'Brown' first appears in the fifteenth century so need not concern us here. The second place-name is **Neenton,** which Gelling says means the settlement by the Neen, a pre-English name of obscure origin for the River Rea, although the Middle English word for a settlement or estate '*tun*' has been added to the older word. The incidence of Neen place-names along the river valley, such as Neen Savage and Neen Sollars indicates how the British river name was perpetuated into the English speaking period. *'Ea'* is Middle English for a river; *atter ea* meaning 'at the river' was then transliterated as *Rea,* the name by which we know the river today.

Ditton Priors (see map on p.*xiii*)

The rest of our place-names derive from Middle English.[37] Most important for our story was the granting of an estate, or *'tun'* to a man called *Doda*, a common name in ninth and tenth century Mercia. *Doda's tun* is the first place-name that we can link with today's village of **Ditton Priors**.[38] Doda was probably a theign or other household official of the King of Mercia and was given the estate as a reward for services rendered and as a means of supporting himself and his family whilst serving Mercia's ruler. It even seems likely that Doda's wife and children would have resided in *Doda's tun* when service took him away. It would also seem that *Doda* was not given the Manor as an outright gift, but rather granted principal tenure, as Domesday Book shows that in 1066 the manor was still in the ownership of the Earl of Mercia.

In addition to Doda's estate **Middleton** is recorded in the thirteenth century as Mittelinton and Muttelton and meant the settlement on the little river junction, which it is. The addition of the suffix 'Priors' will be discussed in Chapter 7. **Derrington** was an estate associated with a man called Deora, whilst **Hudwick** was once the dairy farm of Hudda. **Ashfield**, an original part of Ditton, was an open area characterised by ash trees, whilst **Sidnall** came from two words meaning a 'wide nook' – and today's map shows Sidnall Farm on the edge of a large shallow depression. **Netchwood** is a bit of an enigma, but probably contains the Middle English word *eccels* meaning additional land. By 1086 **Ruthall** was a manor in its own right and may have the Early English element *rot* meaning root, but the jury is still out on its exact meaning.

Ditton Priors' field names still in use can also give an indication of their location, shape, size or ownership in pre-conquest times. Frogs Well is in today's parish of Neenton although it is named in several land charters pertaining to the manor of Ditton in the fourteenth century when it was called *Froche wall* being derived from the Middle English *frosc waelle*. *Brende* in Middleton means burnt land and probably related to the method used for clearing the land for cultivation. The Criftins, also in Middleton, meant the little enclosure, although in medieval times this whole area was an open field system. Again in Middleton, Pudesbache, so called in 1328, meant the valley of the toads. By 1728, the name had been transformed in Pudsbatch. Powkesmore meant the marsh or moor of the goblins.

Place-names of Brown Clee

When the Clee Hill estate was broken up, probably in King Offa's reign, the boundaries of the manors that surround Brown Clee were delineated to ensure an equitable distribution of arable and grazing land as illustrated by the map. Such a distribution could only have been undertaken because the kings of Mercia owned all the land hereabouts.

The smaller manors of the Brown Clee have Middle English place-names that reveal their origins in the centuries before the conquest. **Stoke St. Milborough**, listed as *Godestoch* in Domesday Book of 1086 related to the fact that it was a dependent settlement (*stoc*) of God, or at least God's representative on earth, Wenlock Abbey. **Burwarton**

The parishes around the Brown Clee.
(Drawn by Hugh Bryan)

meant the settlement of the fort-guardian and relates to a pre-Viking time when a defensive system existed in the area, most likely to repulse the Welsh. Gelling (2001) adds that it cannot be a coincidence that seven out of the ten place-names that contain the name *'burf'*, meaning fort, occur in Cheshire, Herefordshire and Shropshire. **Abdon** was Abba's estate and **Cleobury North** was the Manor by the Clee, gaining its suffix 'North' to distinguish it from Cleobury Mortimer. Slightly further away places whose history touches Brown Clee are Tugford, the ford of Tucga whilst Loughton was possibly an estate associated with a man called Luhha. These were the estates that in years to come will share the grazing rights on the Brown Clee.

Using place-names to reconstruct landscape

Place-names evidence supports the contention that the parishes of Ditton Priors, Neenton and Cleobury North were once part of the larger land holding based on the Clee Hills. The map below illustrates how the field name of Harley in Ditton and Hartley in both Neenton and Cleobury North covers an area now lying in all three parishes, whilst 'mill' field names continue into Neenton but archaeological evidence shows that the mill was then, as it is now, in the present parish of Ditton Priors. Both Hartley and Harley share the same derivation, namely 'clearings in the Stag's wood'. However, the great or multiple estate of the Clee Hills must have been divided soon after these names were given as all the new

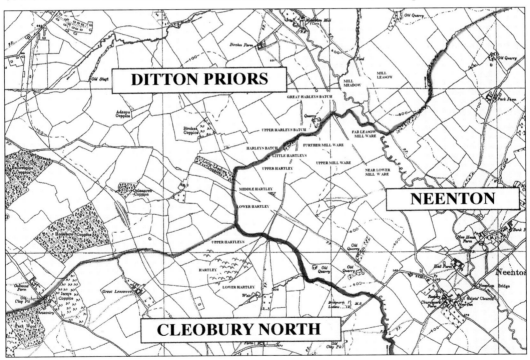

The field-names of Harley and Hartley straddle the parish boundaries of Ditton Priors, Cleobury North and Neenton indicating that the names predate the boundaries. Based on 1954 OS map

manors around the Brown Clee also have Middle English names. Dr. Gelling suggests that the reign of Offa (757-796) is most likely for the introduction of the *tun* place-names, so it also seems likely that this was the period when the great Clee Estate was divided into the manors we know today.

The Boundaries of the Parish of Ditton Priors and Beyond

Fourteenth-century documents show that parts of the manor of Ditton lay in the parishes of Neenton and Monkhopton[39] and it is likely that even in pre-conquest times the boundary of the manor was not coterminous with that of the parish. The 27-kilometre parish boundary of Ditton Priors may not have been finalised until the twelfth or even thirteenth century although Morris (1989) supposes that the church organised parish system was laid out no later than the tenth century. This may be borne out by the fact that Ruthall was detached from the manor of Ditton before the conquest, but remained in the parish of Ditton Priors, as did Ashfield which was detached in the twelfth century. The population owed dues, taxes and tithes to their local church so the demarcation of each parish boundary became an important geographical feature to be known and memorised by all parishioners. All the parish boundaries of Ditton Priors, except those formed by streams, are ditched and banked, whilst some of the boundaries on the hill have additional stone walls on top of an earlier bank. Some of the ditch and bank is most likely to be a pre-Conquest feature.

The County of Shropshire is likely to have been created in Edward the Elder's reign, (899-924) although there is good evidence that Shrewsbury had been a Mercian *burh* with its own military hinterland before Edward became ruler of this part of Shropshire

Netchwood boundary ditch

14

Boundary wall in Cleobury North

in 918. South Shropshire conforms to the land of the Magonsaete and the diocese of Hereford. Such a well-defined and long-established geographical area would have had a cohesive administrative structure with hundred courts in place in Mercian times.[40] Ditton's hundred court in the pre-conquest period was at Patton on the Corvedale Road to Wenlock. Even in the twenty-first century, when Patton consists of a single farm, a direct route can be traced from Ditton via existing roads and public rights to way.

Agricultural life in Ditton

If the hypothesis outlined in these early chapters is correct then the royal houses of the Magonsaete and Mercia directly owned the land later known as the manor of Ditton. Such powerful owners would have given prestige to the tenants of Ditton, although the manor's agricultural way of life would have been much the same as other well-run estates.

Society would have been elaborately graded with slaves at the bottom of the order and freemen at the top, much as outlined in Domesday (see Chapter 5). It is not known when the open field system of arable farming began, but it could have been in place before the conquest with Ditton having three large open fields and Middleton two as in later medieval times. Our Anglo-Saxon ceorls or husbandmen would have used the heavy plough known from Roman times pulled by two or four oxen. It may even be that in our heavy soil, six oxen were needed to make the furrows.

Each tenant farmer would have a number of strips scattered throughout the fields on which they would grow wheat and rye, planted immediately after the harvest, and barley and oats sown in spring. Flax and woad were also regularly cropped in the midlands. Oats were fed to young animals and also provided porridge for human consumption. Barley, the main staple crop, was used for both bread and the beer that the Anglo-Saxons drank in large quantities. In both the fields and gardens of the poor, beans would be cultivated. Agrarian history records a reliable assumption that our Anglo-Saxon population continued to harvest '… the wild and cultivated fruits which had been known in the Roman period, including apples, medlars, cherries, mulberries, plums, bullaces and damsons.[41]

15

Drawing on evidence from Finberg (1967) it seems likely that the meadows situated alongside Ditton's many streams and pastures on Brown Clee, Netchwood, Lightwood and Powkesmore would be highly prized with sheep and goats, rather than cows, being kept for their milk. Pigs were the most numerous animals and would feed on the mast found in the many woods around the village.

The absentee royal landlords of Ditton Priors would have claimed much of the cultivated food and animal products as 'food rent' and this would be taken on the well-organised road network to wherever it was required. Such was the situation until Domesday and beyond.

CHAPTER 4
Mercia's Hunting Ground to Domesday Manor

Aethelred, Earl of Mercia and Aethelflaed, Lady of the Mercians: 885 – 1018

Aethelflaed's statue in Tamworth, the principal Mercian town in the early tenth century

Alfred's organisation of Wessex in the years following his accession in 871 is detailed in the Anglo-Saxon Chronicle which tells of the training of military forces to fight the Danes, and establishment of *burhs* or fortified settlements throughout Wessex so that all inhabitants lived within 20 miles of their protection. Simultaneously, Alfred introduced education with emphasis on the English language. Such a system, the chronicle implied, gave the people of Wessex a unifying framework, which Alfred reinforced by making Christianity the supreme influence on his kingdom. However, it must be remembered that the people of Wessex wrote the chronicle and present day Mercians should not forget the fortifications and military organisation of kings such as Offa that predate Alfred's time.

By the 880s, the ruler of Mercia is named as Aethelred and whilst the chronicle calls him an ealdorman and later an earl, it would appear that he ruled as king and may have been related to the old royal house of Mercia. Evidence to support this contention is supplied by Bassett[42] who notes that in 885, Aethelred was powerful and maybe royal enough to marry Alfred's daughter, Aethelflaed, when she had only just reached marriageable age. Moreover, many joint ventures against the Danes were conducted but Aethelred and Aethelflaed always had sole control of the part played by Mercia in such forays. Important for our story is a document dated 901 in which Aethelflaed and Aethelred are described as '... *Monarchiam Merceorum Tenentes ...',* namely holding the monarchy, or sole rule of Mercia. This charter records Aethelflaed and Aethelred involved in a complicated deal involving land at Stanton Long [43] to the benefit of Wenlock Abbey, proving that Mildburh's foundation was still in control of lands around the Brown Clee and that Aethelred held the allodial, or inherited, lands of Brown Clee previously held by his royal Mercian predecessors. Whatever Aethelred's origins, he and Aethelflaed held joint rule and were instrumental in organising this part of Shropshire in the fight against the Danes.

By the first decade of the tenth century, Aethelflaed and Aethelred had fortified or refortified many of the settlements in western Mercia. *Burhs* were built or rebuilt, including Shrewsbury in 910 and Bridgnorth in 912. Christianity was reinforced with grants to religious foundations such as the one described above. Aethelred died in 911 and Aethelflaed continued to rule alone until her death in 918, when her brother, Edward the Elder, deposed her daughter, Aelfwyn, and ruled what was becoming a united kingdom of the English.

It seems likely that a re-enforcement of the English language took place under Aethelred and Aethelflaed that continued into the rule of Edward the Elder. English was the language of their administration and a uniting factor as it had been in Wessex. This could explain why this part of Shropshire has so few old British place-names when compared to other western counties.

Ditton's Right to take Salt from Droitwich
Another feature of pre-conquest Ditton that can be inferred from the limited evidence available is that both before and after the great estate was divided the Mercian kings and their earl successors used the Brown Clee area as a hunting ground. Great nobles came here with many attendants and slaughtered the wildlife of the area. The game might then be transported to the Mercian capital at Tamworth or some other stronghold, or stored in the area to sustain the next royal visit. The meat would need to be preserved and salt from Droitwich was used for this purpose. Mercian kings and their earl successors held rights to Droitwich salt as evidenced by early charters, such as the one dated *c.*717 when King Aethelbald granted salt rights to the church of Worcester.[44] No salt charter relating to Ditton is known to exist, but it seems possible, even probable, that one of the Mercian kings bestowed the right to take salt from Droitwich on the large estate centred on Brown Clee, and when the estate was broken up that this right was attached to the manor of Ditton Priors, where it is recorded in Domesday Book. It is, of course, perfectly possible that the salt right was granted at an earlier time by the kings of the Magonsaete who were linked with the tribe of the Hwicce who ruled the Droitwich area. But whenever the salt right was granted the theory of using it to salt game appears most appropriate.[45]

It is thought that initially the salt right was linked to manors with the ability to produce vast quantities of wood needed for boiling the brine at Droitwich. It took one cartload of wood to produce 1 mitt (56lbs) of salt and as Ditton was entitled to 24 mitts per year or 1,344lbs, 24 cartloads of wood would be needed.[46] Today's place-names of Ditton

Priors with Middle English origins such as Ashfield, Oakwood, Netchwood, Lightwood and the Birches reveal its earlier wooded landscape whilst the Stag's Wood, mentioned above, covered a large area to the west of Reabrook. In addition many fields to the east of the Reabrook are derived from the Middle English *'bearu'* meaning a grove. Clearly Ditton had no difficulty finding wood for Droitwich.

The Forest of Clee

This right to Droitwich salt and the fact that Ditton was the largest of all the newly formed manors immediately around the Brown Clee (with the exception of Stoke St Milbourgh long since gifted to Wenlock Abbey) gives credence to the belief that in late Saxon times the Forest of Clee was administered from Ditton. Eyton (1860) writing of the Clee Forest says 'In Saxon times I should rather suppose it to have been appurtenant to Ditton, a manor of the Mercian Earls ...'. Indeed, the establishment of the Royal Forest of Clee by William the Conqueror, where only the king and his appointed officials could hunt game, may have prompted the awarding of the salt right, although it is known that such rights were a feature of earlier times. With Ditton being one of only three Shropshire manors with the right to take salt from Droitwich, Caynham and Donington[47] being the other two, and the likely administrative centre of the Saxon Forest of Clee its significance in pre-conquest times must be assumed.

Rowley (1965-66) writes that all documentary evidence indicates that the Clee Forest was limited to the Brown Clee area alone and although it remained under Royal jurisdiction for only a short period its importance lies in the survival of the right of intercommoning enjoyed by the inhabitants of the Brown Clee settlements.[48] This right to graze animals on Brown Clee was also important in medieval and later times.

From Conquest to Domesday: 1066 – 1086

After Aethelred, subsequent Earls of Mercia owned Ditton. Leofric (*c*.1040-1080) and his more famous wife, Godiva, or Godgifu, lavishly endowed Wenlock Abbey, showing they were still involved in the area, but it is Leofric's grandson, Edwin who is recorded in Domesday Book as having owned Ditton in the time of Edward the Confessor in 1066 when it was valued at £10.

At the time of the Norman invasion, Earl Edwin and his brother Morcar owned the three Shropshire salt-right manors of Ditton, Caynham and Donington. But times were turbulent and in 1071 the brothers led an unsuccessful rebellion against the rule of William the Conqueror, and consequently were stripped of their lands. Ditton, along with almost every other manor in the area now passed into the hands of Roger Montgomery, Earl of Shrewsbury, probably a cousin of William, who had been left behind to administer Normandy when the Battle of Hastings took place in 1066. Roger Montgomery arrived in England in 1067 and was immediately given valuable tracts of land including the rape of Arundel in Sussex. It is believed that he was not granted large parts of Shropshire and Herefordshire until after the rebellion of the Mercian earls in 1071 but it is under the ownership of Roger that Ditton gets its first entry into written records in 1086. This Domesday Book entry is discussed in the next chapter.

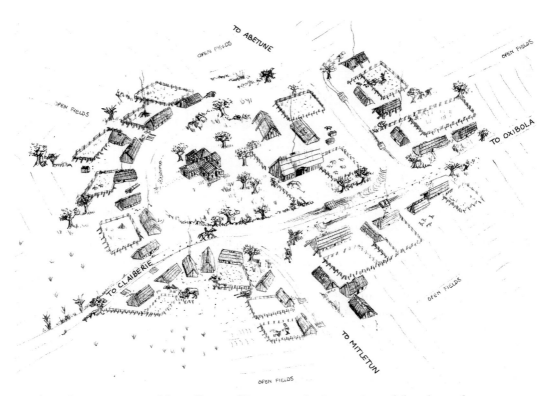

Artist's impression of the village of Ditton at the beginning of the eleventh century. The 'island site' and the road system are in place. (Drawn by Sarah Connor)

From this point on the book will be mainly devoted to this prosperous important manor then called Dodentone, but soon to get its modern name of Ditton Priors.

CHAPTER 5
From Domesday to Hugh de Perriers: 1086 – 1175

The Village of Ditton Priors in 1086

At the time of the Norman Conquest the layout of the village of Ditton Priors or Dodintone as it then was, would have been recognisable to today's inhabitants. The island site is of Anglo-Saxon origin and contained the three principal buildings of the village, namely the lord of the manor's house, the priest's house and God's house, the church. All the clues are in place to make this assumption. First the island site with its three buildings is a known feature of Anglo-Saxon landscape.[49] Second, the present church is principally Norman in construction and yet is more than 17 degrees off an east-west axis, a misalignment that Saxon builders frequently made aiming for sunrise and sunset rather than magnetic north. Normans, who were purists for religious correctness, rarely countenanced such a misalignment unless building on the foundations of an earlier church. Third, the present day church tower bears signs of being the original centre of a previous cruciform church in that signs of a doorway can be seen on the exterior north wall, whilst the internal door into the nave has typical Anglo-Saxon long and short stone work with rounded moulding over the door. The first church on this site may have been built of stone, but is more likely to have been timber-framed. The early lord of the manor's house is also likely to have been on the site of the later one, now known as Church Farm, whilst the priest's house, or vicarage was on the island site until moved in 1828.[50]

The main roads radiating from the island site to all the neighbouring settlements were in existence as they probably had been for hundreds of years. Our ancestors would have used many more subsidiary tracks, some of which exist today as ancient rights of way. The open field system of farming was practised by this time with small 'in-fields' close to the village and three or more large fields further away. These large fields were divided into strips called selions, cultivated by individual farmers. This system features heavily in our later medieval documents but is likely to have been introduced in pre-conquest times.

The Anglo-Saxon 'island site' with its church, site of priest's house and lord's house depicted on the 1768 map of Ditton Priors

Domesday Book 1086

At Christmas 1085 William I commissioned the docu-ment that has come to be known as the Domesday

Ditton's entry in the Domesday Book (Allecto Historical editions, 1990)

Book because the facts it contains could not be disputed and so was likened to the great last judgment. William wanted a survey of the resources he held in order to reappraise royal taxation needed to defend his lands against both internal and external threats. Commissioners were appointed to a number of provincial circuits, courts were held and juries summoned to present the facts about each settlement. The commissioners reported their findings in 1086 and this is what they recorded about the manor of Dodintone.

> Dodintone – Held by Roger, Earl of Shrewsbury
> Earl Edwin held it in the time of King Edward with 4 outliers
> 12 hides which pay tax.
> In Lordship 5 ploughs: 10 slaves
> 20 villagers and 8 smallholders with 6 ploughs
> 13 other ploughs would be possible there
> In Droitwich 1 salthouse which pays 2s
> Before 1066 it paid £10: now £11

Even though the record was compiled for taxation purposes, it reveals several facts about the manor. Taking each entry in order, we learn that in 1086 Roger, Earl of Shrewsbury, held the manor from the king. The Earls of Shrewsbury, Hereford and Chester between them held nearly all the Welsh Marches and were given royal or palatine power to rule this turbulent area. In this respect the owner of Dodintone was second only to the king in power in the immediate post-conquest period.

Edwin, Earl of Mercia, held Dodintone in 1066 and it is this entry that has allowed the development of the theory that the manor's ownership can be traced to rulers of the Magonsaete outlined in previous chapters. The four outliers or townships attached to the manor of Dodintone in 1066 are likely to have been Middleton, Derrington, Hudwick and either Ashfield or maybe Sidnall.[51]

Dodintone paid tax on twelve hides, which is a unit of taxation linked to acreage and there is still much debate as to exactly what constituted a hide in 1086. As a rough guide, a hide may be assumed to be 120 acres and if correct for this part of Shropshire, the entry says that Dodintone has 1,440 acres on which tax was payable.

The next entry 'in lordship' refers to the fact that Dodintone was Earl Roger's demesne land, namely that he did not lease it to an under tenant, but employed a bailiff taking the rents and produce directly for himself. He is reported to have 5 ploughs and again there is debate over the exact meaning of a plough, but is likely to relate to another unit of taxation rather than an implement for cultivation.[52] Earl Roger had 10 slaves to work his land. This reveals that post-conquest England, as with the Anglo-Saxon period before, was a slave owning society, yet by the twelfth century slavery was virtually unknown. Morgan (1988) suggests that many of the slaves may have lived in their own households and held small amounts of land.[53] From this perspective it can be argued that some of Ditton's villagers of succeeding centuries may have been descended from Earl Roger's slaves.

Twenty villagers and eight smallholders are listed and it is probably useful to consider them as holdings or tenancies rather than as individual people.[54] It could be assumed that those listed as villagers or *villani* held their land directly from Earl Roger and owed him services and dues whilst the smallholders or *bordarii* had freehold tenancies. Whatever, the nature of their holdings they had land that paid tax reckoned at six ploughs, but the Domesday commissioners considered that more money, the equivalent to thirteen ploughs, could be obtained from Dodintone. The total population of the manor in 1086, if the usual multiplier of 4.5, is used was *c*.170.

The salthouse in Droitwich has been dealt with in the last chapter. Domesday showed that 2 shillings tax was payable on the salt. This tax is known to be one old penny per mitt allowing for the calculation that Dodintone received 24 mitts, or 96 bushels per year.[55]

The last Domesday entry refers to the income that Earl Roger could expect to receive from his lands. Mill dues were excluded from Shropshire Domesday, as was the value of the royal forests, so the £11 recorded value was just the amount paid to the earl by the inhabitants of Dodintone. Only penny coins were minted in 1086 and so the sum must have been calculated in terms of customary services and dues such as working the land and heriots, namely goods and animals paid to the lord on the death of a tenant. Earl Edwin could only expect to receive £10 in 1066 so Dodintone is worth £1 more in 1086, although there is not enough information to explain why this should be so.

A comparative look at some of the other Brown Clee settlements at Domesday shows that Dodintone had a higher value, larger population and paid more tax than any other manor situated around the hill. Abdon was valued at 12 shillings with a population of *c*.40 including three slaves, Burwarton was worth only 2 shillings with a population of *c*.9 whilst Cleobury North could also muster *c*.40 residents, including one slave, who must pay in coin or kind 20 shillings to Wulfeard, their lord of the manor. Cleobury North is a good example of the complexity of some Domesday holdings, because Wulfheard, a rare English rather than Norman name, held the manor from Roger de Lacy, who in turn held it from the king. The only Brown Clee manor that can compare in value and population with Dodintone is Stoke St. Milborough. It has 20 hides of which 17 pay tax, a population of *c*.150 and a value of £9, although it was worth £13 in 1066. By some deal Earl Roger has given Stoke St. Milborough to his chaplains, but the Domesday Commissioners record that the church, meaning Wenlock Priory, should have it and soon after 1086 the manor was returned to Wenlock, now a priory, who had held it for the last four hundred years and who continued to hold it for another 450 years. Stoke St. Milborough did not contain any slaves because the church discouraged slavery.

The Founding of Wenlock Priory

About six years before Domesday Book was compiled, Roger, Earl of Shrewsbury founded the Priory of Wenlock. In the seventh century, Wenlock had been a double monastery, later abbey, with Mildburh as its second abbess. In the eleventh century Earl Leofric of Mercia and Godiva had lavishly re-endowed it, but Earl Roger's foundation or re-foundation made the institution into a priory. The earl had a deep regard for the Abbey of Cluny in France, which had pioneered Benedictine reform, and he requested that monks from Cluny come to Wenlock. The Grand Abbot of Cluny passed the request to Cluny's daughter house at La Charité-sur-Loire who provided the first prior and monks.[56] The priory of Wenlock inherited the lands held by the pre-conquest abbey and during the next century were given several more manors, including the wealthy manor of Dodintone. This story must wait until the next chapter, although it is useful to note that in the centuries after Earl Roger's foundation, the priory became ever more rich and influential.

Soon after 1100 a monk called Goscelin arrived at Wenlock with the specific intention of writing down the history of the priory and its saintly abbess, Mildburh. Goscelin was a professional hagiographer[57] and using what he claimed were original early charters penned *The Testament of Saint Mildburh* discussed in Chapter 2.[58] Goscelin's account substantiated the ancient traditions of the monastery, re-enforced the cult of St. Mildburh and most importantly for Wenlock confirmed the possessions that the institution had held since her time.

In 1110 and 1115 conferences were held at Westminster and Castle Holdgate to ascertain the status of Wenlock Priory and its large land holdings. The result was a charter which was to affect this part of Shropshire for the next seven centuries, namely that all the land belonging to St. Milburga's Priory constituted one parish and was subject to the mother church in Wenlock.[59]

Dodintone becomes a Royal Manor

Earl Roger died in 1094 and, as was the custom of the time, his second son Hugh succeeded to his English earldom whilst his eldest son, Robert inherited the Normandy estates. Robert had already inherited the French lands of his mother, Mabel de Belleme, and with his father's inheritance he became the most powerful magnate in Normandy, a position he used to oppress all those who opposed him which included the king of England. Orderic Vitalis, a contemporary historian, described Robert as tyrannical in that he terrorised the Belleme lands in Normandy including the monastery where Orderic lived.[60] Hugh, Earl of Shrewsbury died in 1098 and Robert immediately took possession of the English lands claiming them as his inheritance. Robert's rebellion against King Henry I in 1102 probably came as no surprise and his supporters' final stand against the king's forces in Bridgnorth ended in his defeat. This resulted in exile and confiscation of all the Earl's English lands that his father had held which are listed in Domesday. Ditton or Dodintone along with many other Shropshire manors became a crown possession for the next fifty years. These were the years of the English civil war between Stephen, the nephew of Henry I who had succeeded to the throne, and Matilda, Henry's daughter who claimed what she saw as her inheritance. The fighting only ceased when Stephen and Matilda reached an agreement that Matilda's son, Henry, would inherit the throne on the death of Stephen.

CHAPTER 6
From Crown Estate to Wenlock Priory: 1155 – 1300

Hugh de Periers, Lord of the Manor: 1155 – 1175

Hugh, from Periers-sur-Andelle in Normandy, first entered written records in 1153 when he was one of the signatories of a charter signed at Coventry. The donor named in the charter was Henry Duke of Normandy and Aquitaine and Earl of Anjou, the future Henry II, who at this time was still fighting for his inheritance.[61] It seems that Hugh de Periers was one of Henry's French supporters and at this time hopeful of a reward for his service.

Henry II succeeded to the throne in December 1154 and by the following September had granted Dodintone along with two other Shropshire manors, Corfham and Culmington, to Hugh de Periers. These three manors gave Hugh a yearly income of £42,[62] Dodintone still being worth the £11 per year recorded in Domesday. Ashfield had been detached from Dodintone in the time of Henry I and given to the Beysin family who held it by service of keeping the king's hawk.[63] The ditch and bank boundaries of Ashfield, whilst clearly delineated, are neither so wide nor so deep as those of Ditton and Ruthall, confirming that they were created at different times. Two 'mere stones' or boundary markers remain on the bank, one on the south side at Ditton and the other on the west at Stanton Long, as they must have done for the last few hundred years. After the Norman Conquest, all land was decreed to belong to the king and the king's vassals held it by virtue of some kind of service, usually a commitment to provide fighting men if or when called upon to do so. The Beysins would appear to be fortunate in that they only had to provide hawks, although the keeping and training of hunting birds was an expensive business, and it may not be a coincidence that Ashfield is adjacent to the hunting ground of the Clee Hills.

Hugh de Periers does not enter the written records again until the end of 1175 when feeling death approaching he created a charter which, as was the custom of the time, made arrangements for his soul, his wife and his retainers, in that order. In the hope of eternal life he gave to the priory of Wenlock his manor of Ditton, to Alice de Cheney his wife, he left a life interest in Ditton stating that only after her death should the Prior take full possession of the manor. To his retainers he reserved their rights to the lands they held in Sidnall and Middleton, stating that they should continue to hold these lands of the priory under the same terms as had been agreed with himself.[64] Soon after this charter was written, Hugh died at Wenlock Priory and was buried within its walls.

Despite Alice de Cheney having a life interest in the manor, the monks lost no time in coming to some sort of deal with her so that by 1177 they had received a charter from Henry II confirming that Ditton was now in full possession of the priory.[65] But the monks were not to get their hands on Ditton so easily. Alice, Hugh's widow, married Geoffrey de Say and by 1180 it would appear that he had reseized the manor by force,

Part of the land charter dated c.1260 in which John the Woodward granted land in Middleton. The names highlighted are the field-names of Deneway and Puddesbache, both of which can be found in today's landscape. The seal on the charter reads John of More, called John the Woodward in the document. John's grandson and his descendants assumed the surname of Forester. (SA 6000/9663)

as the Forest rolls of that year show Geoffrey is fined two marks for making waste in Hudwick and Ditton. No doubt this gave Geoffrey a good bargaining stance with the prior who by the end of the year is again confirmed to be in full possession of the manor of Ditton, but only by payment of 160 marks and an annuity of £14 per year to Alice for the next eight years.[66]

Two witnesses of the charter by which Hugh de Periers gave Ditton to Wenlock in 1175 have a Ditton interest. Adam Pincerna, or Adam the Butler, and Walenger are two of the four vassals or retainers of Hugh de Periers to whom land in Middleton and Sidnall was enfeoffed.[67] This meant that Hugh had detached part of the manor of Ditton and given 'tenancies in fee' to his retainers. Each tenant would have had a legal charter confirming the grant and after Hugh's death they paid a rent or gave a specified service to their overlord, the Prior of Wenlock, but were free tenants which meant that they could sell or sub-let the holding as they wished. From the mid thirteenth century, this land is the subject of a succession of charters whose landholders bear names that can be associated with Hugh's retainers. These documents give the medi-

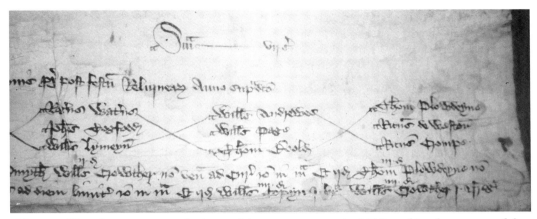

Thomas Plowden serves on the jury of the manor court in 1412 and is also amerced for not hedging his fields (SA 1224/2/6)

Today Ardesley is marked on the map as Horseley Wood. The deed was written at Cleobury North and dated the Feast of the Annunciation 23 Edward III, namely, 25 March 1349, and has a seal attached. Clearly some Brown Clee people were doing well in the 1340s despite war, famine and disease.

By the 1370s the priory received just over £9 in combined rents from Ditton tenants who were obliged to provide customary services and from free tenants who simply paid rent, plus 6 shillings and 8d. from the mill.[89] This sum is less than the amount Roger of Montgomery received in 1086. However, like many other lords of the manor, the Prior of Wenlock was introducing new forms of tenure. Rather than manage the whole estate, landholdings were now leased to tenants. Copies of the leases were enrolled in the manor courts, and some, but not all customary services were subsumed into the rent. These copyhold tenancies would become the norm for all priory lands until the mid sixteenth century and the monks came to rely on the rents for the support of the priory. Thomas of Plowden was granted such a copyhold tenancy of land in Ditton in 1364[90] and either he or his son appear again in the records of 1411 when Thomas Plowden was not only a juror in the manor courts but was also fined for not building a hedge around his strip of land (see illustration above).[91] Whilst the copyhold tenancies made their holders more secure, customary services such as carriage duty, heriots payable on death and the extortionate tercier system continued to be claimed by the lord of the manor.

Throughout the fifteenth century the manor now appeared as Dytton on most documents and hereditary surnames became the norm allowing us to follow the fortunes, or otherwise of our Ditton residents. No description of this century would be complete without a mention of the Smallman family who feature so largely in the history of Ditton Priors. On Sunday 27 November 1418, the first Smallman appears in the documents when Richard Smallman witnessed a deed relating to land in Middleton. In the first decade of the sixteenth century we know that William Smallman, demesne farmer of Ditton,[92] was the bailiff of the Prior of Wenlock and it may be that his predecessors also worked for the priory in some capacity. Smallmans were well settled in Ditton Priors by 1468, the year of

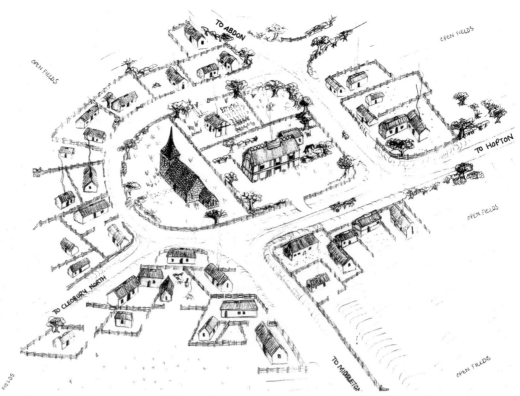

*An artist's impression of Ditton Priors at the beginning of the fifteenth century.
(Drawn by Sarah Connor)*

*Richard Smallman (as highlighted) makes his first entry into the records
of Ditton Priors in 1418 (SA 6000/6990)*

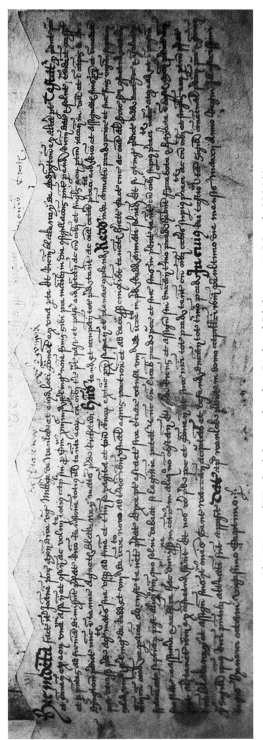

*The Prior of Wenlock leases land to Richard Blakeway in March 1535/6.
The deed was signed in the chapter house at Wenlock (NA E303/14/247)*

the earliest minute book of the newly chartered town of Wenlock. On the very first page 'Richard Smallman of Dytton' was present as well as John and Thomas Smythe, also from Ditton.[93] These men were burgesses of Wenlock that would exempt them from paying market tolls when they took their produce to town.

The copyhold tenants of Ditton Priors increased in wealth and status and by the beginning of the fifteenth century a full rent roll shows eleven principal tenants in Ditton, headed by William Smallman, three in Derrington, fourteen in Middleton and one each in Sidnall and Hudwick. The total rent received for the standard tenancies amounted to £25 6s., but several farmers were paying rent for newly assarted land that added another 12s. 11½d. to the yearly amount received by the priory. The accounts in 1510 identified the rent paid by Ditton tenants as part of the kitchener's rental, namely that the money was allocated to whoever held this office at the monastery. [94]

The lives of the sixteenth-century people of Ditton were well regulated. Petty offences and breaches of the code of communal farming were taken before the manor courts,[95] whilst offences against God's law, which were deemed to imperil the health of ones soul, were taken before the ecclesiastical or church courts. Thus we learn that in 1530 John Marks, who according to the 1510 rent roll lived at Hudwick, was reported for saying profane and blasphemous words in the lands of the church. Roger Nicholls and Ann

Barratt found themselves reported for adultery in 1534, as did Richard Holland and Alice Grey. Poor Agnes Smythe was reported as being pregnant by a certain Thomas Hoggekes of Rushbury and in 1539 was ordered to perform the full penance of appearing in church in a white shift, prostrating herself on the floor and begging forgiveness of God in front of a full congregation.

Agnes Smythe and the rest of Ditton would have been aware that great changes were in place. Richard Blakeway who was granted the lease of lands in Ditton Priors in March 1535/6 may also have wondered just how long his landlord, the Prior of Wenlock, would survive.[96]

Smaller monasteries had begun closing in 1532 and in 1534, Henry VIII had made himself supreme head of the church in England thus supplanting the Pope. From 1536 onwards the larger monastic institutions were suppressed and on 26 January 1540, in the Chapter House of Wenlock Priory, the monks signed the deed of surrender, allegedly confirming that '… they had freely and spontaneously given and granted …to our most illustrious and invincible prince and lord Henry the Eighth … all that our said monastery … ground, circuit ... precinct and church of the said monastery with all our movable debts, chattels and goods … and all and singular our manors, lordships, messuages…to be alienated, given, exchanged or transferred to any uses whatsoever agreeable to his majesty.'[97] By such a deed was the manor of Ditton Priors and all the other manors transferred directly into the hands of Henry VIII. This would be the fourth time that Ditton Priors had belonged to royal rulers, but this time it was to stay in the king's hands for only four years.

CHAPTER 8
Manor of the Pakingtons: 1544 – 1600

The Pakingtons buy Ditton

After the dissolution of Wenlock Priory, Henry VIII directly owned the manor of Ditton Priors and its revenues went to the Crown, but on the 23 August 1544 the manor was sold to a London mercer with Worcestershire roots, Humphrey Pakington. A great number of such manors were on the market at this time and Humphrey paid the relatively small sum of £644 16s. 8d.[98] It is clear from the purchase deed, or Letters Patent, that Humphrey had bought not only the land but the tenants as well.

The Letters Patent detail his assets: -

> ... all and singular the messuages, mills, tofts, cottages, houses, buildings, lands, meadows, feedings, pastures, woods, underwoods, rents, reversions, services, charged rents, suit rents, … fee farms, annual farms, annual rents, waters, fisheries, fishings, furse, heath, common moors, marshes, ways, empty spaces, male

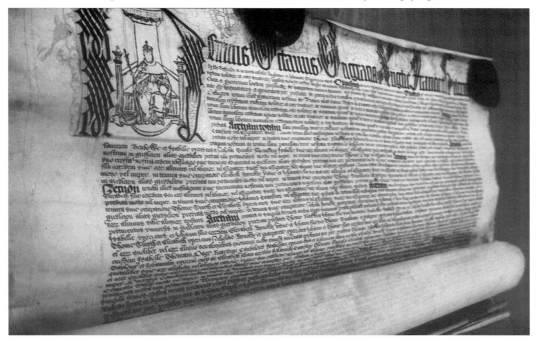

Letters Patent by which Humphrey Pakington bought the manor of Ditton Priors from King Henry VIII. The deed was witnessed by Queen Katherine (Parr) (SA 422/1)

and female natives and villeins with their children, knights fees, wards, marriages, escheats, reliefs, heriots, fairs, markets, tolls, customs, courts leet, profits of courts and perquisites of courts, view of frankpledge, strays, tithes, glebes, rights, profits, commodities, emoluments … lying or being in the vills, fields, parishes or hamlets of Middleton, Derrington, Dytton, Powkesmore and Hudwick …[99]

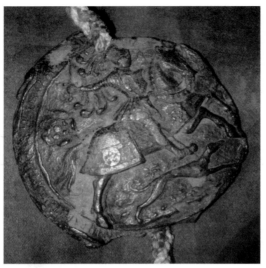

The seal of King Henry VIII on the Letters Patent (SA 422/1)

Each principal tenant is listed and where he was a copyholder whose wife, children or grandchildren could inherit the lease, they too are listed. William Smallman was still the demesne farmer of Ditton:

> … our capital messuage with appurtenances in Ditton aforesaid being now or lately in tenure or occupation of William Smallman and Thomas Smallman his son and John and Richard sons of the same Thomas Smallman …' [100]

With few exceptions the people named in 1544 were the same or descendants of those in the 1510 rent roll and many of the surnames would still be there in rent rolls of the following centuries.

Humphrey Pakington also bought the advowson, the right to appoint the vicar to the church. This is the same right that the Prior of Wenlock had possessed and meant that the great tithes went to the lord of the manor with only the small tithes going to the vicar.

The social and agricultural life of this century is described in the manor court rolls detailed in the next chapter and it may be that gentry farmers such as the Smallmans, Reynolds and Hollands with their copyhold tenancies saw little change in their day to day dealings with the lord of the manor and his officials. But the old order had changed and this would have been most visible in the church and its services.

The Changing Church

Throughout the early medieval period the interior of Ditton church was plastered and limewashed[101] and probably covered in colourful paintings. Attendance at church was compulsory and villagers would have stood in the nave listening to the priest intone the mass in Latin behind the rood screen separating the nave from the chancel. Henry's break with Rome and Edward VI's drive to establish a Church of England without Latin liturgy, painted walls and statues of saints, created a much altered church. In 1547, the vicar, William Alcocke, together with the churchwardens Richard Gery and John Fowler, and two parishioners, John Russell and John Taylor, made a list of the fineries belonging to the church, most of which would soon be discarded. They recorded two chalices, one of gold and one of silver, one cope of blue satin and red velvet, two pairs of vestments, one of red satin and one of white fustian, and three tablecloths and three towels. They also had to admit in their record that they could not produce the old inventory, as it had been lost.[102]

In the same year the chantry chapel within the church of Ditton Priors was abolished. Chantries were established to enable priests to say masses and prayers for the souls of benefactors and their ancestors. Unknown founders had endowed Ditton's chantry known as the service of Our Lady, with lands that were now sold to benefit the Crown. At its dissolution the chantry was valued at £2 4s and 8d. Three years later John Smallman was recorded as being in possession of 'one parcel of land inclosed with hedges called St. Mary Held formerly belonging to the service of the Blessed Mary of Ditton ...'.[103]

The new rites of the Church of England were proscribed when Queen Mary came to the throne in 1553 and it is certain that one of our villagers was not pleased with the attempt to re-introduce the rules and services of the Church of Rome. William Alcocke, the vicar of Ditton who compiled the list of church goods in 1547, found himself arraigned before the Bishop of Hereford in 1554 because he had married Elizabeth Reynolds of Ditton Priors.[104] The record does not record William's punishment, but he is likely to have lost his living.

Elizabeth I's accession to the throne in November 1558 ensured a return to the liturgy of the Church of England. The early years of Elizabeth's reign were marked by tolerance to Roman Catholics, a situation that would not last two decades.

The Lords of the Manor

The Pakingtons, whose principal residence was Harvington Hall in Worcestershire, had been purchasing lands in Shropshire and Herefordshire from the early 1520s. After 1540 they bought several whole manors that had previously belonged to various monastic houses. Ditton was no doubt intended to be a good investment, but there is evidence that each successive Pakington who inherited the manor lived here for some of the time and became involved with Ditton people.

Humphrey Pakington I, who died in 1556, left £10 to the poorest of Ditton and another £10 for mending the highway between Ditton and Bridgnorth. Ten poor maidens in Ditton were to receive 10s. on their marriage, and his servant, Richard Reynolds of Ditton, was left £5.[105] One other bequest should be noted for he left to 'Adam Lutley, my Steward at Ditton and my loving friend, £5'. The Lutleys lived at Broncroft Castle, a few miles from Ditton and would feature in the history of Ditton Priors for the next two centuries.

Humphrey's eldest son, another Humphrey, predeceased his father, so the second son John inherited the manor of Ditton and all the other Pakington lands. For the next 20 years Ditton became wealthier with more land taken in for cultivation from the surrounding wastes such as Netchwood and Powkesmore. By the time of John's death in March 1578[106] a great change in the earlier religious tolerance was underway due to the perceived threat from Roman Catholics inside and outside the realm. By 1580 Jesuits and other priests were infiltrating English society and old Catholics and new converts were labelled as recusants and subjected to intense scrutiny and anti-Catholic laws. It was a serious offence to harbour Catholic priests and many of those who did so were linked to treason plots and suffered sequestrations of their property, all of which affected our next lord of the manor.

Humphrey Pakington III: 1578 – 1631

Elizabeth Pakington, John's widow and Humphrey[107] III's mother, was the first Pakington to find herself under suspicion of being a Roman Catholic when in 1580 Bishop Whitgift of Worcester recorded her for absenting herself from church for the past year.[108] In 1585 Humphrey, his brother John and their three sisters made the first of many entries into the recusant records and by 1591 Humphrey's Shropshire estates had been sequestered[109] and leased to the lawyer William Seabright, Town Clerk of London and a Member of Parliament for Droitwich. The period of sequestration lasted until 1606 and netted the sum of £431 13s. 4d. for the Exchequer.[110] Humphrey's freedom to travel was seriously curtailed and he was placed under house arrest at Harvington Hall, although in 1595 he was ordered to London to face the Privy Council 'to th'end he may have conference with som learned devines to work him (if possibly yt may be) to some conformity'.[111] Clearly Humphrey would not be turned for he remained steadfast to the Roman Catholic faith for the rest of his life. Such adherence meant fines, which he never paid, and further house arrest. There is no evidence that he ever acted treasonably against Elizabeth, although Harvington Hall is famous for its priests' hiding places installed by Humphrey and his equally ardent Roman Catholic wife, Abigail.[112]

Throughout the period when Ditton Priors was under the sequestration order, its steward, Adam Lutley, the son of Humphrey I's loving friend, continued to administer

Humphrey Pakington and his second wife Abigail. Humphrey's portrait was painted in 1599 whilst Abigail's dates to the 1620s. (Photographs from reproductions at Harvington Hall, originals in Coughton Court)

Harvington Hall, Worcestershire, renowned for its priestholes, the home of Humphrey and Abigail Pakington who were responsible for their creation

the Ditton Priors estate. Adam's son John married Humphrey III's sister, Mary, and they had eight children. One of these, another Adam, became the next steward of Ditton Priors whilst his brothers, Humphrey and Philip, became Roman Catholic priests with Humphrey serving at Harvington Hall in the seventeenth century.

The sequestration of Ditton Priors may not have been as serious as it appears. When William Seabright died in 1620 he left £30 to 'my most loving and kinde kinsman Humfry Pakington'.[113]

The Catholics of Ditton Priors

Despite the early legislation of Edward VI and Elizabeth which aimed to strengthen the newly established Church of England, the earliest recusant records to be found for Ditton residents only begin in 1587, when parishioners were charged in the church courts with absenting themselves from church because they were 'in Popish error'. It is not surprising that Catholics found themselves targeted by an ever-vigilant administration, for this was the year of the execution of Mary Queen of Scots and the threat of a Spanish invasion, which duly came the following year. By 1588, the number of Ditton people named as recusants in the church courts reached record numbers, although it would appear that some residents of Ditton Priors were not targeted by the church, for the names of John Bullock, gentleman, of Sidnall and John Longfield, yeoman, of Ditton can be found in the list of recusants only in the Pipe Rolls of 1591-92.

Thomasina Crowther is the first Ditton name in the recusant list, but Nicholas Smallman senior, and Nicholas Smallman junior, and their entire families appear with such regularity and over such a long period of time that they stand out as the most overtly Catholic family in the parish. It is almost certain that they lived in the house known today as Hyde Farm. Both Nicholases refused to baptise their children or allow their daughters to marry in church although no doubt such ceremonies were performed elsewhere by Catholic priests. The whole family of Nicholas Smallman was excommunicated which meant that not only were they barred from receiving holy communion in the local church, something that clearly would not have concerned Nicholas, but it also meant that none of his neighbours could communicate with him. John Smith of Derrington was charged with such an offence when he was taken before the church courts in 1606 for 'keeping company with Nicholas Smallman a recusant excommunicated person.'

An entry in the church court records of 1605 reads: -

> Nicholas Smallman hath entertained in his howse Samuel Smallman his brother who doeth refuse to com to churche.

This Samuel Smallman must be Humphrey Pakington's priest ordained in Rome in 1603, and who died in a fall from a horse in 1613 while serving at Harvington. His name heads the list of Roman Catholic priests in the entry vestibule of today's Roman Catholic chapel of Harvington Hall. In view of Humphrey's involvement with the manor of Ditton, it seems likely that not only did he protect and pay the fines imposed on the Smallman family for recusancy, but he also paid for Samuel to go to Rome for ordination.

Humphrey Pakington III died in 1631 and in the decade before his death the Smallmans were continually reported to the church courts by the local informer, whose name is given as John Capper, for offences such as slandering relatives, clandestine marriages, employing excommunicated people and in 1622 Francis Smallman is reported for calling his sister-in-law a 'rave troaden whore'. This is the decade of the rise of the godly gentry and it is possible to imagine that, with an elderly and often absent Lord of the manor whose only heirs were two teenage daughters, the informers were exercising their power by harassing their Catholic neighbours.

The church courts also hint at tension within Ditton Priors between the Protestant Smallmans,[114] which included John and Richard, and the Catholic family that included Nicholas and Francis. The following entry may refer to this feud, or it just may illustrate what a belligerent lot the people of Ditton were at the beginning of the seventeenth century: -

> John Smaleman, son of Richard Smaleman reported for calling Thomas Reighnolds knave arrand paltrie knave roge rascall, villaine and had stoke him with his fist if Thomas Woodward had not heed and hindered him in the churche of Ditton one Sundaie the 13 Aprill 1600.

The Elizabethan age was nearly over, but the Catholic villagers and their lords of the manor were to face more troubles in the centuries ahead.

CHAPTER 9
Sixteenth-century Economic and Social Life

The Manor Courts

The manor court regulated the agricultural and much of the social life of the manor of Ditton Priors. Only six court rolls are known from the entire fourteenth and fifteenth centuries, but thirty-seven survive from 1510 to 1614 and although there is an uneven coverage of the period, they allow an unparalleled glimpse into the lives of the then Ditton residents.[115]

The Ditton courts were of two different kinds.[116] Until 1570 only courts baron were held dealing with surrenders of tenancies, transfers of land, the agricultural administration of the commons and wastes, the rights of tenants and lords of the manor and the enforcement of customary rights and duties. From 1570, with a few exceptions the courts were called view of frankpledge[117] and court baron, and these administered statute law, minor criminal offences as well as the custom of the manor.

The main settlements of the parish, Ditton Priors, Middleton nearer Ditton, Middleton Further (today's Middleton Bagot) and Derrington appear in every court roll, whilst the smaller townships of Hudwick and Sidnall make irregular appearances.[118]

The leading free and customary tenants, usually numbering twelve, were sworn in before each court and these jurors both heard and presented cases. The constables of each

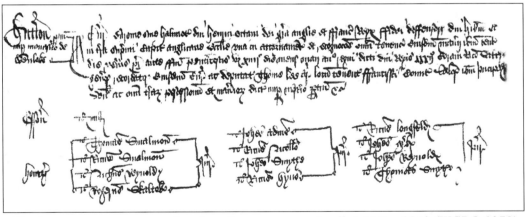

The homage or sworn men (jury) on the manor court roll, 14 May 1540 (WCRO 1379)

Thomas Smalman	*John Adams*	*Richard Longfield*
Richard Smalman	*Richard Nicolls*	*John Markes*
Nicholas Reynoldes	*John Smyth*	*John Reynoldes*
Roger Skaltoke	*Richard Hyns*	*Thomas Smythe*

The present Church Farm, built in 1578 – but erected on the site of an earlier manor house where manor courts may have been held

settlement also presented inhabitants who had infringed various codes of conduct or they reported that all was well in their township. Two other tenants were appointed afferors who established the amount tenants were amerced (fined) for transgressions. From 1572, the courts were presided over by Adam Lutley, the Steward, who was followed in that office by his sons-in-law, first Edward Littleton and then George Holland. The courts may have been held in church, being the largest building in Ditton, or outside if the weather was fine. In the later half of the sixteenth century they may have been held in the open hall part of the building now called Church Farm. Such a building would have been known as the Manor House and dendrodating reveals a felling date for the timber of 1578.

Agricultural Life and Death Matters

By far the greatest number of court entries relate to the management of the open field system that had already existed for several centuries. Animals had to be kept off the sown fields by means of movable hedges made of brushwood or similar, and hardly a court goes by without an entry such as: -

> Margaret Fowler for having her hedge in decay at Bent Furlong ... she must repair and amend the same by Lammas next under the pain of 10s. (1576)

Margaret had to pay 6d. for the decayed hedge and another 6d. for storing a hedge at Oak Wood. Similarly, Richard Nicolles had not repaired his hedges at Pyrlefield – today's Hall Farm Road – and was amerced 8d. (1548) The importance of safeguarding the growing crops was recognised by an entry in 1570 when John Crowther was amerced 12d. for driving his cattle over the open field of Pudsbache after the field was 'heyed and sown'. He was ordered not to take his team (of oxen) that way again under pain of 3s. 4d.

Any notion that agricultural matters would not proceed normally after the dissolution of Wenlock Priory were dispelled when Thomas Jefferies was granted tenure on the death of his father 'according to the form, effect and tenor of his indenture granted to him under the common seal of the former prior and convent, former monastery of Wenlock.' However, the king intended to claim all the rights including the tercier on the death of a tenant as the prior had before him. On the death of Thomas Jefferies senior, the court roll details what is due to the lord of the manor, in this case Henry VIII.

> ... one animal in the name of his heriot price 8s. and other goods and chattels ... to wit; 6 piglets price 3s. 4d.' 2 stalls of bees price 2s. and a brass pot price 8d. (1541)

It would seem the king was happy to accept the money rather than the animals and the brass pot.

In 1577 we know that flax and hemp were grown in Middleton because Richard Reynolds and Ellen Crowther, widow, were reported to have polluted the stream by washing these items. They came to an agreement with the lord concerning the amercement, namely two hens or 16s. Pollution of the stream at Derrington was brought to the attention of the court in 1591/2 when John Smith reported William Blakeway for washing cloths in it. Blakeway responded by reporting John Smith for similarly polluting the stream by allowing his geese to swim there. The court made an order, or pain, that both men should not pollute the stream in future. The dispute clearly rumbled on for more than a decade, as in September 1614 the jurors ordered that Widow Blakeway and John Smith should have use of the stream for alternate months. As this is the last manor court roll in the series, subsequent ones being lost or destroyed, we do not know if this even handed approach resolved the matter.

Encroachments and Illegal Enclosures

With each tenant farmer having strips in the open fields the courts were kept busy ensuring that one tenant did not encroach onto another's land or onto the common grazing pasture.

> They (the jurors) present that Richard Tench has enclosed a parcel of land, part of the common called le Heth Lane (1527)

Such was the need for cultivated land that Heth or Heath Lane (now called Sandy Lane) was not the only road in danger from the ploughman. In Middleton Priors Richard Candland had '... for two years with his plough changed part of a common way leading between Shrewsbury and the town of Bewdley and planted flax thereon.' (1535)

On many occasions the jurors had to appoint some of their number to adjudicate on disputed boundaries such as encroachments on the Bent (1572) and those at Oldfield (1605). One entry confirmed the boundary dividing Middleton next to Ditton from Middleton Further, when in 1604 an order was given to inquire into the muck and carrion in the '*stream between the 2 Middletons*'.

The Commons and Wastes

By the custom of the manor and copyhold tenancies the number of animals that each tenant could graze was strictly regulated. Generally speaking the common grazing land for Middleton tenants was Netchwood and Lightwood whilst Ditton residents grazed Powkesmore and Brown Clee. Those with customary access to Brown Clee were also subject to the Swainmote, an ancient intercommoning agreement with all the other manors that surround the hill.[119]

Grazing rights were valuable. John Hyntes, Margery his wife and Thomas their son paid 20s. and a yearly rent in 1546 for an indenture that allowed them to graze six beasts in Powkesmore, a right that had previously belonged to the late Nicholas Smallman. The tenants of the Manor of Ditton jealously guarded their rights, especially when a grazing ground such as Netchwood was shared with another parish, in this case, Monkhopton. The ditch and bank that separate Ditton's Netchwood from that of Monkhopton is still clearly visible today.

> A pain is placed on all the tenants of Hopton and Weston who have enclosures called swine sties in the wood of the lord of Netchwood that they shall remove the same swine sties before the feast of St Michael the Archangel next under pain on each of them of 20d. (1547)

The maintenance of roads and tracks to drive the beasts to the grazing ground also concerned the manor courts: '... William Page ... shall immediately well and sufficiently make the gate called the Outrackyate..' (1549)

The health of the grazed animals on the commons was important. In 1530, John Wylde is presented by the jurors because he has '... put a scabby mare called reyffe on the common pasture to the harm of all the neighbours.' And in 1595, one colt, the possession of William Catstree deceased, was brought to the court's attention because it was on the common and was less than 14 hands high. This relates to a statute of Henry VIII whereby horses less than 14 hands were not encouraged to breed as larger horses were needed for the armoured men of the day. A trawl through the manor courts of Ditton Priors illustrates how laws or statutes passed by parliament were enforced through the manor courts.

Offences Against the Statutes

An Elizabethan statute of 1571, designed to promote the wool trade, forbade the wearing of hats on Sundays. Only woollen caps could be worn. Ditton's yeoman farmers clearly thought the wearing of such apparel beneath their dignity. For the next two decades, whilst the law was in force, they readily acknowledged their superior social class by wearing a hat not a cap and paying the 4d. amercement.

> Nicholas Bullock of Sidnall ... presents that he is in mercy of the lord for his hat worn on feast days and Sundays against the form of the statute. (1577)

Poaching or any act that could contribute towards the destruction of game features in many statutes. Cottagers found themselves in court for keeping a dog (1576), tracking hares in snow (1597), shooting a gun (1602). Earlier, in 1552, Walter Waters was amerced 12d. for taking and killing hares by means of 'instruments called harepipes'. Earlier still (1540) William Bent had been described as a 'common waster and taker of partridges with traps nets and an engine in distraction (*sic*) of the warren ...'. He was amerced 6s. 8d.

In 1528 Henry VIII had issued a proclamation,[120] incorporated into statute law, whereby the playing of games, be it football, bowls or cards, was outlawed as they were deemed to prevent practising archery with longbows, the only approved recreational activity for young people. Improvements in ordnance had clearly advanced by the end of the sixteenth century and bows were no longer the principal weaponry of warfare. However, this did not prevent our young men being taken before the courts for failure to practise at the butts. In 1599, the whole township of Ditton was presented at court because '... they do not have sufficient butts for archery ...'.

The Manor of Ditton Priors was under a sequestration order in the 1590s because of Humphrey Pakington's Catholicism, and all profits went to the crown, so it may be that the many and various amercements imposed on the population under statute law was an attempt to boost the coffers of the exchequer.

Social Life

The social life of our ancestors was as strictly regulated as the agricultural one. In 1535 an order was made that '... all the tenants of Ditton selling ale must not allow any men to play at dice in their houses except on the feast of the birth of our Lord, under pain of 13s.'

The playing of illegal games continued to be brought before the courts as well as such diverse matters as orders to repair ruinous houses; evictions of 'inmates', namely lodgers taken in by the lord's tenants without permission; and 12-year-old boys coming to court to swear allegiance to the queen. Tensions within the villagers are brought to light by the many entries relating to assaults that appear in the last decades of the sixteenth century. All English manor court rolls record assaults and amercements imposed for fighting, but in Ditton the church court records the names of local Catholics and it is possible to recognise these villagers and their Protestant neighbours in some of the hostilities recorded in the manor courts.

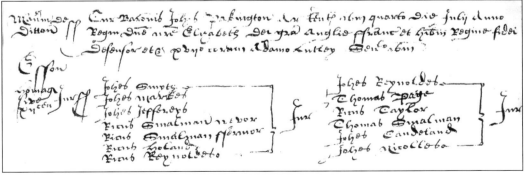

'Court baron of John Pakington held there the fourth day of July in the 17th year of the reign of our lady Elizabeth by the grace of God queen of England, France and Ireland, defender of the faith etc. before Adam Lutley, steward there' (WCRO 1379)

Sorting out the various families of Smallmans can sometimes be difficult, especially when faced with an entry such as: -

> ... Nicholas Smallman, farmer, made an attack on Richard Smallman, butcher ... and ... Nicholas Smallman, farmer made an attack on John Smallman, sexton of said parish. (1589)

In this instance Nicholas the farmer, is a Catholic, whilst the fact that John is the church sexton speaks for itself. Nicholas and his son, also Nicholas, and his grandson, George, who all livied at Hyde Farm, made frequent appearances in the court records for assault and other breaches of court discipline. The inter-fighting between Ditton Protestants and Catholics would rumble on for another three hundred years.

Wills and Inventories

Less than a dozen sixteenth-century wills survive for the parishioners of Ditton Priors.[121] Given that in general only the wealthier citizens made wills they reveal both comfortable living and farming practices for such people. John Smythe of Middleton (d.1578) left to Ursula his wife, a feather bed, coffers and candlesticks as well as flax and 'ten ells of flax cloth' (about 13 yards) whilst his four children got £30 each. Roger Marks (d.1583) left money, pots and silver spoons and to Nicholas Marks 'all manner of things belonging to husbandry at my house at Mytleton (except the Oxe harrow).' The wills of two widows show that their wealth was also tied up in agriculture. Agnes Page (d.1587) left 'corne and grayne in the barn and corne and grayne growing and upon the ground'. Margery Hassall (d.1598) left to Robert and Mary, the children of her son William, one yearling cow. It seems likely that William had predeceased his mother as all other goods were left to her daughter Eleanor.

Both sixteenth and seventeenth century wills reveal the inter-marriages between village families. The will of Agnes Page (d.1587) names her brother, Thomas Reighnolds. John Crowther's will (d.1573) refers to his son-in-law, John Nicholls, whilst the will of Roger Marks (d.1583) recorded: -

> I give to Jane Hotchkiss six Pounds thirteen shillings fower pence which I promised to give her when I married her mother.

Nicholls, Reighnolds or Reynolds and Hotchkiss are Ditton Priors' surnames.

The Church Courts

The recusancy of the Roman Catholics was not the only transgressions dealt with by the ecclesiastical court. Canon law was used to hear cases that involved moral and sexual misconduct as well as proving wills, which had been church business since the thirteenth century. The courts could not impose physical punishments or fines but used excommunication, public penance and the humiliation that accompanied it as their traditional sanctions. In cases where guilt was not clear-cut, alleged transgressors were allowed to

46

bring compurgators to court to affirm their good character.[122] From 1510 to 1630, the court records of the Deanery of Stottesdon[123] show that the parishioners of Ditton Priors were brought before the registrar for any behaviour that could be deemed to imperil their immortal souls.

Sexual misconduct in one form or another can be found in almost every one of the 120 years of records. In 1534, Edward Ree and Dorothy Acton were reported for sexual relations outside marriage. Edward brought John Jeffries and Thomas Smallman as his compurgators and the case was dismissed. In the same year Henry Esthope of Dytton and Johanna Geffrees were reported for the same offence. This time the compurgators were Richard Holland and Thomas Geyrs. Women too fell foul of church rules and the unmarried, but pregnant; Alice Carter's entry in 1534 shows her to have been reported to the court by John Capper. This Capper appears in many entries and was obviously one of the means by which details of wrongdoing reached the ears of the church. It is by his hand that the sexual transgressions of Thomas Alcoke and Beatrice Holond were reported in 1542, although three years later, Beatrice Holand was reported to be pregnant by John Yevans. Henry Capper, clearly a relation of John's, reported John Smallman and Jane Awkockes (probably Alcocke) in 1545 for similar misdeeds.

Any condonement of extra-marital relationships was also frowned upon. John Myles senior was reported for encouraging the behaviour of Edward Myles and Margaret Granaryng who was reported pregnant by Edward in 1545. The clergy were not immune, as the vicar, William Ward, is reported for the 'crime of fornication' in 1560. In 1583, the same vicar appeared as witness when Ann Smallman, wife of Nicholas 'uttered insulting words' to him.

Most of these cases were heard in local churches – Ditton Priors, Neenton, Cleobury North and Ludlow were regularly mentioned – but in 1571, John Hintes and his wife Margaret Butler had to appear at Richard's Castle because they had not had their marriage banns called in Ditton Priors' church. They were required to do penance in the church of Ditton Priors, which involved making an abject apology before the whole congregation. In an age when clandestine marriages were illegal, the calling of banns was deemed essential. Another public penance was imposed on Elizabeth, wife of the Catholic Francis Smallman, in 1622. Unfortunately her original offence is not known, but the report of her re-appearance in court states that 'she did not her penance before the whole congregation at the usuall time of divine service but before the vicar churchwardens and others of the parish before the usuall time of day', so she was ordered to go through the whole procedure again in front of all her neighbours.

Excessive usury was a crime the church courts dealt with as John Jenkes gentleman of Sidnall, found to his cost in 1589 when he lent John Nichols of Ditton £11 and charged 30s. interest.

Some tantalising details of families are found in the court records when wills were proved. The executors of Richard Blakeway, namely John Blakeway his nephew and Nicholas his son, went to court in 1530 to prove the will of Richard, and more than thirty years later, Richard Smallman's executors, Nicholas and William did likewise, unfortunately the records contain no information about the proceedings or goods involved.

By the late 1630s the hold of the church courts over parishioners appeared to be as great as in the previous century, and Ditton Priors inhabitants can still be found in the last few records. In 1631 the first and only entry that could refer to witchcraft was recorded when Elizabeth, wife of Thomas Nicholls, and her daughter Margery, were reported for pretending that they could detect hags, namely witches. Thomas presented a petition whereby he absolved his wife and the case against her and their daughter was dismissed. Another village character was taken to court in 1639 when Catherine Jefferes, wife of John, was reported for being in the company of Lewis ap Owen and drinking in an ale house at the time of evening prayer. The report concluded that she was admonished.

CHAPTER 10
Manor of the Audleys and Barkers: 1631 – 1724

New Houses and Yeoman Farmers

Despite Humphrey Pakington III's personal and financial difficulties, many houses were built or rebuilt during his lordship.[124] Nationally, it was the time of great rebuilding when goods were taxed more heavily than land and houses, hence the investment in both the latter.[125] Houses such as Church Farm (dendrochronology date[126] 1578) and Chapel Cottage (dendochronology date 1553-1585) were timber-framed and only later encased in dhustone, whilst some seventeenth-century houses had dhustone walls from the beginning.[127] The growth in well-built houses reflected a section of Ditton society that became more affluent. In 1628, twenty parishioners were wealthy enough to pay tax and ten of them paid tax on land rather than goods[128] showing that even though the lord owned most of the manor, there were a number of other landowners. These independent owners, plus the freeholders and secure copyhold tenants are likely to have wholly or partly funded the building of their houses.

The seventeenth century saw the beginnings of an agricultural revolution in Shropshire although it took some time to reach Ditton Priors, where strip farming within the open field system continued into the eighteenth century.[129]

By the 1660s, inventories of the wealthier farmers reveal prosperity, but not substantial riches.[130] Oxen were the preferred draught animals and farmers such as John Corfield of Ruthall (d.1667) had 6 oxen and 22 other cattle worth £45 10s. whilst Arthur Lowe's inventory of 1663 recorded 4 oxen, 4 kine, 2 two-year-old beasts, 1 four-year-old beast, 2 mares and 3 swine valued at £49. In the parish, but not in the manor of Ditton Priors, John Taylor's inventory taken at Ashfield on 3 August 1674, revealed 4 oxen and 4 cows valued at £28, whilst his 3 swine were only worth 10s. each.[131] The paucity of swine, reflected in these and other inventories, probably indicates that pannage in the open woods had declined. When William Smallman died in 1681 he left 12 oxen, a working bullock, 10 cows, 8 weanling calves, 6 yearlings, 7 two year old horses, 1 nag, 2 mares, 4 colts, sheep, swine, geese and other poultry as well as 'wayne yoakes plowes and other ymplements of husbandry'. Smallmans were still the leading farmers of the manor and William's goods valued at £191 15s. 10d., showed him to be one of the wealthiest of Ditton's farmers. In contrast, when William Pugh died in 1706 he owned only a few clothes and 8 sheep worth £1 4s.[132] This single illustration of the widening gap between the wealthier inhabitants and their poorer neighbours becomes more marked in the following centuries.

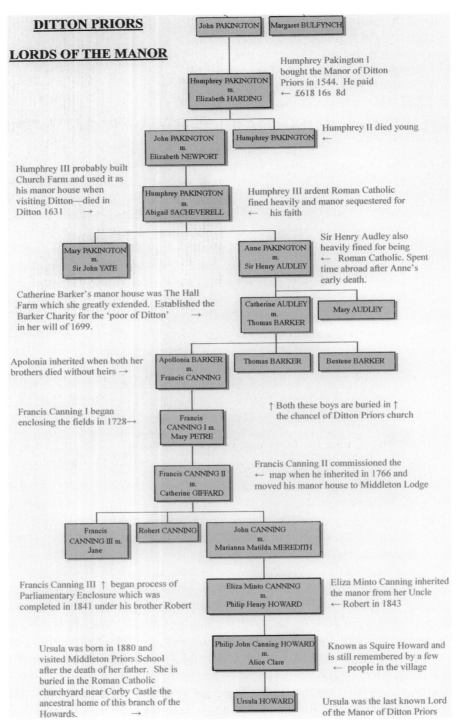

DITTON PRIORS

LORDS OF THE MANOR

John PAKINGTON — Margaret BULFYNCH

Humphrey PAKINGTON m. Elizabeth HARDING

Humphrey Pakington I bought the Manor of Ditton Priors in 1544. He paid ← £618 16s 8d

John PAKINGTON m. Elizabeth NEWPORT

Humphrey PAKINGTON

Humphrey II died young ←

Humphrey III probably built Church Farm and used it as his manor house when visiting Ditton—died in Ditton 1631 →

Humphrey PAKINGTON m. Abigail SACHEVERELL

Humphrey III ardent Roman Catholic fined heavily and manor sequestered for ← his faith

Mary PAKINGTON m. Sir John YATE

Anne PAKINGTON m. Sir Henry AUDLEY

Sir Henry Audley also heavily fined for being ← Roman Catholic. Spent time abroad after Anne's early death.

Catherine Barker's manor house was The Hall Farm which she greatly extended. Established the Barker Charity for the 'poor of Ditton' → in her will of 1699.

Catherine AUDLEY m. Thomas BARKER

Mary AUDLEY

Apollonia inherited when both her brothers died without heirs →

Apollonia BARKER m. Francis CANNING

Thomas BARKER

Bestene BARKER

Francis Canning I began enclosing the fields in 1728→

Francis CANNING I m. Mary PETRE

↑ Both these boys are buried in ↑ the chancel of Ditton Priors church

Francis CANNING II m. Catherine GIFFARD

Francis Canning II commissioned the ← map when he inherited in 1766 and moved his manor house to Middleton Lodge

Francis CANNING III m. Jane

Robert CANNING

John CANNING m. Marianna Matilda MEREDITH

Francis Canning III ↑ began process of Parliamentary Enclosure which was completed in 1841 under his brother Robert

Eliza Minto CANNING m. Philip Henry HOWARD

Eliza Minto Canning inherited the manor from her Uncle ← Robert in 1843

Ursula was born in 1880 and visited Middleton Priors School after the death of her father. She is buried in the Roman Catholic churchyard near Corby Castle the ancestral home of this branch of the Howards. →

Philip John Canning HOWARD m. Alice Clare

Known as Squire Howard and is still remembered by a few ← people in the village

Ursula HOWARD

Ursula was the last known Lord of the Manor of Ditton Priors

From the Pakingtons to the Howards – the family tree of the lords of the manor

The Lords of the Manor

When Humphrey Pakington died in 1631, he left two teenage daughters. The youngest, Ann, had married Sir Henry Audley of Essex in 1628 when Humphrey had settled his Shropshire manors of Ditton Priors and Berrington[133] on her and her husband as part of their marriage settlement. Sir Henry was a professed Catholic for most of his life[134] and suffered the usual penalties, but as Ann was lord of the manor, Ditton Priors did not appear in the list of Sir Henry's sequestrated property.[135]

Sir Henry, finding difficulties at home, took a course followed by many Catholic gentry in the 1640s, he applied for and was granted leave to travel abroad. This was a dangerous time for Catholics who often appeared synonymous with supporters of Charles I who, in 1642, fought the first engagement of the Civil War at Edgehill. Sir Henry left his wife and five children at Harvington with Ann's mother, Abigail, but by the end of 1642, Lady Audley and two of their children were dead. The three

Ann Audley, daughter of Humphrey Pakington who married Sir Henry Audley in 1628 when she was 15.
The manor of Ditton Priors formed part of their marriage settlement.
(Photo: Coughton Court)

remaining children – Catherine, Mary and Thomas – remained at Harvington in the care of their maternal grandmother. In a postscript to a letter written to his mother-in-law in 1645, Sir Henry writes: -

> I must acknowledge your favour in the tender care you have of my son. I hope I shall in short time be able to render the charge you have been at for his breeding, which I humbly thank you for. The county of Salop I hope will pay all ere it be long, if there be anything to be had.[136]

Sir Henry had been absent for some time and the letter implies he was not fully conversant with the affairs of Ditton Priors. Thomas, the surviving son, needed care for in November 1663, he 'became a lunatic', with a guardian committee appointed to look after his interests.[137] It is not recorded whether Thomas was ever endowed with Ditton Priors, but with his death in 1676, having survived his father by only four years, his two sisters Catherine and Mary jointly inherited Ditton Priors.

Catherine had married Robert Barker of Essex, another Roman Catholic, but by the 1690s she was a widow and she and her children spent much time in Ditton Priors. By 1693 she had extended the residence now known as The Hall Farm but recorded as The Hall until the mid-eighteenth century. Catherine died in 1700 leaving £5 per year payable

The certificate in the National Archives showing George Smal(l)man
of Middleton paying tax because of his Catholicism (NA E115/382 & 381)

from the estate to be shared amongst the poor of Ditton, a custom that continued until the 1950s.

Three of Catherine's sons are buried in Ditton church: Robert (d.1689), Thomas (d.1704) and Bestene (d.1705) were buried in the chancel where Thomas's and Bestene's gravestones can still be seen. There is no vault under the chancel, and the floor would have been dug up and maybe a brick-lined grave made to take the bodies. Thomas and Bestene must be assumed to be Roman Catholics, but as lords of the manor they owned the chancel and so could make such arrangements. Neither left an heir and when Bestene died their sister, Appollonia, who had married Francis Canning of Foxcote in Warwickshire, inherited the half share of the manor. Mary Audley, Catherine Barker's sister, held the other half. She died unmarried in 1724 when Francis Canning, son of Francis and Appollonia became lord of the united manor of Ditton Priors.

The People of the Manor

Documents of the first half of the seventeenth century show the continued presence in the parish of the Catholic Smallmans. The will of Francis Smallman of Middleton dated 3 May 1624 has the preamble: -

> ... in the two and twentieth yeare of the reigne of our Sovereign Lord James by the grace of God of England, Scotland France and Ireland, King, Defender of the true ancient Catholic and Apostolic faith and Jesus Saves.

Without doubt a Catholic will although the church courts granted probate. Francis goes on to leave to '... Mr Humffrey Pakington, gent ... my dear landlord four pounds.'

By this time, the persecution of Roman Catholics had taken the form of an increased taxation for those wishing to profess the Catholic faith. In 1628 and 1633, George Smallman, of Middleton,[138] was subjected to a Residency Certificate indicating that he had paid this higher tax because of his Roman Catholicism.[139]

In 1642, the year of Lady Audley's death, the puritan parliament organised a protest against 'an arbitrary and tyrannical government', namely the perceived Catholic leaning regime of Charles I. All male Englishmen over the age of 18 were required to take the 'protestation', although many Catholics refused. One hundred and eleven inhabitants of Ditton took the protestation, including eight Smallmans. Francis Ellis, described as a popish recusant, was Ditton's only refusal.[140] Nicholas Smallman and five Hassoulds or Hassalls, another recusant family, appeared on the protestation return so they either squared their consciences or maybe felt too unprotected to refuse.

The protestation indicates a population of around 345,[141] but it is the only record of the Civil War years relating to the people of Ditton, so we do not know how the inhabitants fared during this time.

During the Restoration period the Catholic Smallmans appear to have either conformed or left the parish, as the Religious Census of 1676 shows only three Catholics and three non-conformists, likely to be the Hassalls and Yopps mentioned below.[142] It was only at the end of the century that overt persecution of Catholics ceased, and it would be many more years before the Catholic Emancipation Act of 1829.

The Parish Officers

After the dissolution of the monasteries, Ditton Priors was placed in the Franchise of Wenlock for the administration of official local government business. Each quarter or half year, parish officials presented their reports and accounts to the Bailiff and Recorder of Wenlock. From 1657 the survival of these presentments show both the holders of the various offices, leading citizens of the parish, and the tasks they undertook in the organisation of parish affairs.

The Village Constable was probably the oldest parish office as its equivalent can be found in 1256. The manor courts elected village constables and they were responsible for keeping law and order within the manor. Wrongdoers were either presented to the manor courts or dealt with by the parish. By the seventeenth century, the duties of constables were becoming detached from their manorial origins in that many miscreants had to be taken before the justices. As no magistrate lived within the manor of Ditton Priors, this meant either a trip to Much Wenlock, or later in the century taking cases to Henry Mytton of Cleobury North. The seventeenth-century constable had a wide range of duties including upkeep of the stocks and the punishments that went with them, supervision of itinerant beggars and the reporting of recusants and non-conformists. Thomas Page, Constable of Middleton for 1662/3[143] dealt with all these issues: -

1. Noe felonies have been committed within my liberties.
2. Noe vagrant persons or sturdy beggars have past through my liberties but 3 such were whipped and stocked and sent by a pass to ye parish of Neene Savage to ye best of my knowledge.
3. I present Thomas Hassall and his wife and William Hassall theire sonne al above ye age of sixteen for Popish recusants and for not coming to church for the space of 3 months.
   Also I present John Yopp and Mary his wife for not coming to church for this 3 months past.[144]

The return of William Taylor, constable of Ditton Priors at the same session shows a similar concern with law and order: -

I have whipt and stocked two several persons and sent then to the place of their last legal settlement.

I also present Arthur Reynolds, William Reynolds and Francis …? For making a most notorious affray & for desperately wounding one John Cassle as by the relation of severall people hath been told me.

By the eighteenth century the inhabitants of Ditton Priors had either become more law abiding or the constables did not go seeking wrongdoers, as reports are not so detailed. The report of Daniel Cross, constable of Middleton Priors in 1737 is typical in that he says he has nothing to present, but returns Thomas Millichop and Henry Morris of Derrington and Daniel Cross of Middleton to serve on juries.

Highway Surveyor's report for 1657 mentions taking more stone to Plowdens Bridge

Plowdens Bridge today – could it be named after the fourteenth- and fifteenth-century Plowdens who farmed this area?

The Highway Surveyor post was created in 1555 when the Highway Act introduced unpaid statute labour on the roads for four days a year, later increased to six, under the supervision of an unpaid officer appointed by the parish. All able-bodied men were forced to provide this labour service and received nothing more than drink and bread for the work undertaken. In January and June, the Highway Surveyors, one each from Ditton and Middleton, had to attend special highways sessions of the justices to report on the conditions of the roads in their area and to present the parishioners who had not performed their statutory labour duties. In 1654, during the Commonwealth, an ordinance allowed parishioners to impose a highway rate of not more than one shilling in the pound to be spent on road maintenance. Shropshire records show that Ditton Priors was one of the first parishes to take advantage of this Act, for in 1657 the Highway Supervisors of Ditton and Middleton made their reports. Thomas Hammonds for Ditton presents Edward Holland of Sidnall for not paying his highway tax, but with the money raised he paid Francis Smallman, mason, for paving in the highways and paid Edmund Power for the carriage of ten waine load of stone and '… disburst for the carriage of more stone to plowdens Bridgg the some of one shilling and two pence.'[145]

William Page of Middleton reports that he has

55

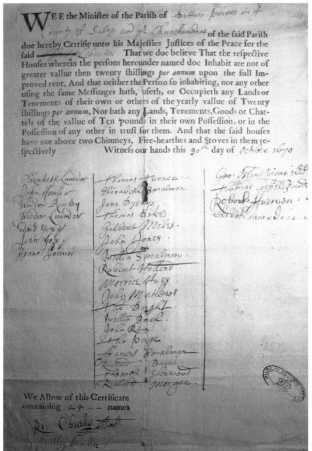

Not all Ditton residents were wealthy enough to pay the hearth tax of 1670 (NA E179/342/1)

'… gathered a peny a pounde of the sevrall inhabitants w'thin the said Township w'ch amounteth unto 18s. 4d. and over that I and others that keepe teems have carried stone w'th out teems diverse days unto the high ways.'[146] Excavation has shown that several rights of way in today's parish are paved and it may be that Francis Smallman, mason, undertook the work.

The Tax Collectors of Ditton Priors were kept busy in the years after the restoration of Charles II in 1660. Fifty-three parishioners are listed on the Lay Subsidy Roll of 1661, amongst them, 6 yeoman, 5 husbandmen, 10 labourers, 1 tailor, 1 collier, 1 blacksmith and 1 gentleman. One year later another tax was levied, named the Free and Voluntary Present to His Majesty King Charles II. It is not known just how free and voluntary this taxation was, but fifty-one residents of Ditton contributed various amounts. Catholic George Smallman of Middleton gave £1 whilst Thomas Sherwood, collier and George Dudlick, Weaver, gave the more usual sum of 1s. From 1662 the government introduced new methods of taxation with a levy based on the number of hearths in each dwelling. The 1672 record reveals that Middleton Priors, including Derrington, was the wealthier township as thirty-three inhabitants paid 6s. 4d. for their 62 hearths whilst the twenty-nine inhabitants of Ditton with fifty-one hearths paid 5s. 2d.[147]

The land tax and window tax of the following century was well recorded, but with few exceptions only names are given allowing limited success in linking taxpayers with

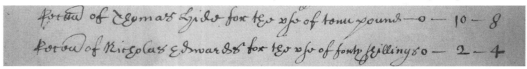

Overseers of the Poor Accounts, 1655, showing interest on money lent by the Overseers (SA Q1/13/22)

56

their properties. A typical Ditton Priors land tax record is the one of 1714 when 2s. in the pound was levied on goods. Twenty-six entries relating to Ditton Priors are recorded, part of which reads: -

George Adney, vicar	£1	02	00	(vicarage by churchyard)
William Smith	£6	00	00	(Ditton Farm)
John Miles for The Hall	£2	00	00	(The Hall Farm)
Francis Palmer	£2	12	00	(Church Farm)
Humphrey Mullard	£1	08	00	
John Miles of Brook	£1	10	00	(Possibly Brook Cottage)
For Jeffries Tenement	£1	02	00	
Charles Wall for Lutleys	£0	16	00	(Botwood)
John Garbett for Powkesmore	£0	08	00	(Powkesmore Farm)
Joseph Reynolds for Lime Works	£0	04	00	(On Hillside)
The occupiers of the mines	£0	16	00	
Edward Holland, gent	£2	06	00	

The recusant roll of 1716 and detective work allows some identification of habitation placed in brackets after the sum paid.

Overseers of the Poor were established in 1597/8 and made compulsory by the Elizabethan Poor Relief Act of 1601. Ditton Priors elected two overseers, one each for Ditton and Middleton at the Easter vestry meeting. Money for outdoor poor relief was collected from inhabitants (in 1655 13s. was collected from money lent by the overseers at c.5% interest, see illustration p.56) and supplemented by the parish possession of a

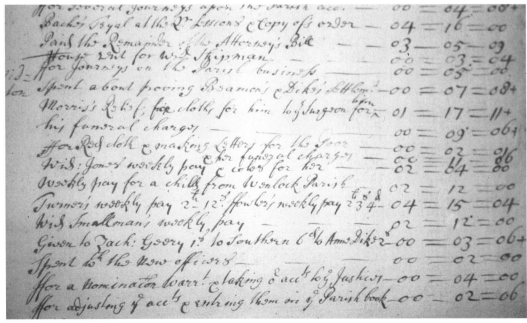

Overseers of the Poor Accounts, 1710 (SA Q1/13/92)

herd of cattle that was rented out. The keeping and rental of 'parish stock' was a fairly common practice, the cattle being left to the church in parishioners' wills, or purchased by the churchwardens from bequests. The sale of paupers' goods on death also added to the coffers. Widows and 'base born' children feature in all accounts: 'To Widow Williams by weekly pay and looking to her being darke and helples £5 4s.' (1704/5). 'To looking to Widow Bach in a hopeless condition' (1711/12). 'For Joseph Bridwell towards keeping the base child for 26 weeks and the Baptism fees 1s. 4d.' (1711/12).

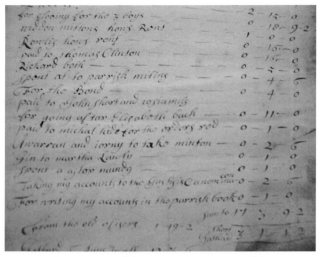

Overseers of the Poor Accounts, 1735
(SA Q1/13/95)

The parish of Ditton Priors was responsible only for those born in the parish and money was spent by the overseers travelling to Wenlock for settlement orders that would return paupers to their place of birth. 'For two warrants and bringing Walford Beamon and Dike before the Justices to prove their settlement 5s. 6d.' (1710/11).

Seamstresses were kept busy, 'For 5 yards of flannel thred and making a garment and coat for Bess Lawley 1s. 8d.' (1711/12). 'For red cloth and making letters for the poor 2s. 1d.' (1710/11). This last entry refers to making large letter 'P's', representing 'pauper', which some recipients would be obliged to wear on their clothing. Poor law relief for many was intended to be stigmatising and Ditton Overseers obviously ensured that for some it was. Concern for the 'deserving poor' can still be discerned in the records, such as the 1735 entry for a woman probably suffering from a painful terminal illness: 'Gin for Martha Lawley - 1 shilling' (see illustration above).

The Churchwardens, appointed each year, were also parish officers of long standing. Originally such appointments were necessary to manage parish property and income and over the years their duties had grown to include amongst other things, responsibility for upkeep of church fabric, allocation of pews and the reporting of any failings on the part of the incumbent. The parishioners traditionally elected one warden and the vicar appointed the other. The churchwardens' accounts for Ditton Priors do not begin until 1786 and will be referred to in a later chapter.

Joseph Holland, shoemaker, Netchwood Common Ditton Priors, with Thomas Holland shoemaker of Much Wenlock, binding themselves on 8 June 1786 [for] Francis Holland of Much Wenlock, father of a bastard child. Joseph, Benjamin and Francis to indemnify the parish of Much Wenlock. The mother being Sara Pugh.[158]

The archives for the Franchise of Wenlock include several of these 'bastardy bonds' for Ditton parishioners. Shropshire's Calendar of Prisoners' also contained a number of Ditton inhabitants: -

13 Jan 1794 - John Morris aged 28, charged upon the oath of Henry Goode of Ditton Priors with a violent suspicion of having feloniously taken, stolen and carried away from the outbuildings and other premises … eleven live fowl.

John Morris was imprisoned for one month and fined 1s. The name Henry Goode appeared again 23 years later, but this is likely to be another Henry: -

26 November 1817 – Henry Goode for refusing to find sureties for his appearance to keep the peace towards Anthony Fryer, Mary his wife and Sarah his daughter. Committed for trial.

Jan 12 1818 - Henry Goode aged 28, a labourer born in the parish of Ditton Priors charged upon the oath of John Jordan of the parish of Burwarton petty constable of that parish accused of violently assaulting him, beating and kicking him.

Tantalisingly the records do not tell us if, or how, these crimes are linked and neither do they reveal the outcome. One that does was the case of William Humphreys: -

July 13 1818 - William Humphreys aged 21 ... of Ditton Priors, labourer, charged on oath of Thomas Cocks .. of Munslow, farmer, on violent suspicion of having feloniously robbed him of country bank bills the value of £19 1s. on Tuesday 12 May last.

One week later William Humphreys was sentenced to seven years transportation to Australia.
    Some Calendar of Prisoners entries are heartrending: -

27 December 1825 - Mary Jones aged 23 … of Ditton Priors charged on oath of having secreted her delivery of a male bastard child on 12 December 1825 [and] secretly buried the child in a garden at Cleobury North.

Mary was discharged by proclamation a week later.
    Throughout this period, the Barker Charity gave out yearly amounts. Accounts exist from 1770 when Widow Clinton, John Garbett, Widow Fowler, Thomas Smallman, and Thomas Rea, all old Ditton Priors' surnames, appeared as beneficiaries before the end of the century. At the beginning of the eighteenth century the sum was usually 5s. payable

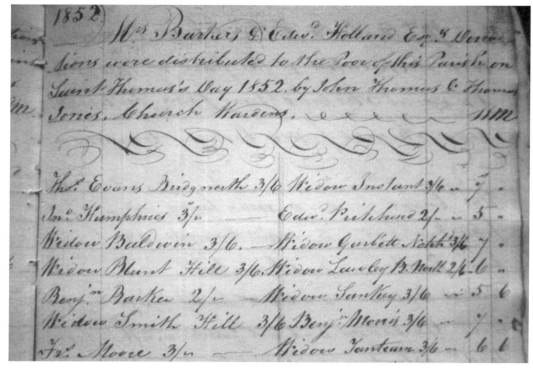

List of recipients from the Barker Charity for 1852

to the poor on St. Thomas's day, 27 December. In the nineteenth century the handout was reduced to 2s. 6d. or less and in later Victorian times just bread and coals.[159]

Knatchbull's General Workhouse Act of 1723 and Gilbert's Act of 1782 encouraged parishes to provide workhouses for the 'impotent poor', such as vagrants, illegitimate children and some aged infirm people, whilst able-bodied parishioners were provided with employment outside the workhouse. The workhouse regime was known as 'indoor relief' and doles to the able-bodied, or those considered the more deserving poor, 'outdoor relief'. Ditton clearly did not waste any time after these Acts were passed as by the end of the eighteenth century it had its own workhouse with around eight paupers being housed there and another thirty receiving outdoor relief in 1815.[160]

When the Victorian Poor Law of 1832 was passed, life became even tougher if that were possible. From 1836 Ditton was part of the Bridgnorth poor-law union and Ditton's paupers were housed in St. Leonard's Workhouse. Four Ditton paupers were resident in the workhouse in 1837: Jane Oakley aged 77, William Goode aged 6, Sarah Morris aged 8 and Eliza Morris aged 13. Eliza was offered to whomsoever would take her on as a servant. Outdoor relief was still payable but only at 11 o'clock on a Wednesday in the Canning Arms (later re-named Howard Arms) for the parishes of Ditton Priors, Neenton, North Cleobury, Stanton Long and Burwarton. The names of those attending for relief in 1836 read like a roll call of Netchwood and Hillside cottagers: Jesse Bache and Ann his wife, Edward Bache and Elizabeth his wife, Edward Lawley, Sarah Massey, John

Margaret Netchwood's birth as recorded in the parish records

Bowen, Thomas Evans and Mary his wife. The last couple attended the poor law officer to receive 1s. 6d. per quarter for fostering a girl called Margaret Netchwood then aged 3.[161] Margaret was christened in Ditton Priors church on 13 June 1834 and the note beside the entry reads: 'A foundling left at a cottage door at Netchwood on the night of the 11 June. In 1841, Margaret was fostered with the Cartwright family and in the 1851 census she is recorded as a servant at North Farm, Middleton Priors.[162]

ANNO SEXTO

GEORGII IV. REGIS.

****

Cap. xlix.

An Act for amending, maintaining, and improving the Roads from *Bridgnorth* to *Cleobury North*, and also through *Ditton Priors* to the *Brown Clee Hill*, and from *Cleobury Mortimer* to several Places therein mentioned, and other Roads branching therefrom, in the Counties of *Salop* and *Worcester*.   [2d *May* 1825.]

The 1825 Act of Parliament to turnpike the road from Ditton Priors to Bridgnorth

Turnpike Road: 1825

On 2 May 1825 a parliamentary Act was passed for 'amending, maintaining, and improving the Roads from Bridgnorth to Cleobury North, and also through Ditton Priors to the Brown Clee Hill, and from Cleobury Mortimer to several Places, therein mentioned, and other Roads branching therefrom, in the Counties of Salop and Worcester.' The Act limited to two the number of tolls that could be imposed between Bridgnorth and Ditton Priors and such tolls could only be paid once a day. Cleobury North and Ditton Priors Trust borrowed money to surface the road and to build tollhouses at Harpswood and Lightwood to collect the two tolls allowed. Accounts for 1825 show that £207 11s. 3d. was expended on the venture of which £34 10s. was interest on a debt of £690. The accounts do not say how this money was used, but it seems likely that it was expended on road surfacing and the employment of gatekeepers and other staff. Another £20 was added to the debt for arrears of interest not paid. The Act prescribed the amount that could be charged: -

> For every horse, or other Beast drawing any Coach, Landau, Chariot, Curricle, Berlin, Phaeton, Chaise, Calash, Hearse, Gig, Chair, Stage Coach, Caravan or Van ... the sum of Sixpence;
> For every horse or other beast drawing any Waggon, Wain, Cart, ... having the fellies of the Wheels thereof of the Breadth or Gauge of Six Inches or upwards from Side to Side at the Bottom or Sole thereof, the Sum of Four-pence; and of less Breadth than Six Inches, the Sum of Seven-pence;
> For every drove of Oxen, Cows, or Neat Cattle the sum of One Shilling and Three-pence per score, ...
> For every Drove of Calves, Swine, Sheep, Lambs, or Goats, the Sum of Ten-pence per Score ...

With so many roads and trackways between Ditton Priors and Bridgnorth, it seems likely that alternative routes were found. Maybe for this reason the venture did prosper as ten years later the total debts were recorded as £2,894 13s. whilst the income from tolls for 1835 only amounted to £345 11s. 4d.[163]

Parliamentary Inclosure: 1805 – 1841

The cottagers probably felt that matters could not get worse, but at the beginning of the nineteenth century Francis Canning began the process whereby the remaining commons on Clee Hill and Netchwood were enclosed. The parliamentary bill was passed in 1801, but due to the death of several commissioners, the land was not surveyed until 1813 and the act not enforced until 1841 when Robert Canning, Francis's brother, had inherited. Six hundred acres, mainly of commons and wastes amounting to one-ninth of the parish was now lost to the cottagers, 373 acres on Brown Clee and 227 at Netchwood.[164] Some of the small freeholders received allotments in exchange for their rights of common, including Samuel Smallman at Lower Netchwood, Edward Bowen at Upper Netchwood and John Blount on Brown Clee. But many cottagers received nothing from the inclosure and now had no means of keeping grazing animals.

The Inclosure Act abolished both the small tithes paid to the vicar and the great tithes paid to the lord of the manor and consequently the largest amount of previously common land was allocated as recompense to the vicar and Robert Canning as impropriator. Henry George Mytton of Cleobury North also benefited from inclosure, he was allocated three acres on Brown Clee because he claimed lordship of the Clee. His claim can be traced to Mytton's purchase of Clee Chase from Sir Humphrey Briggs, last recorded lord of Clee Chase in 1709.

Lords of the Manor

The Cannings were absentee landlords throughout their 120-year holding of the Ditton estate. Foxcote manor in Worcestershire was their principal residence, but they owned property elsewhere. In 1745 Francis Canning bought the house known today as Middleton Lodge[165] from the Hassall family. In 1771 the building was extended and Arthur Lowe given the principal tenancy of 'All that messuage tenement and dwelling house part whereof hath lately been erected and built at Middleton'. The deed goes on to state that a malthouse had also been built and that Canning had a room and parlour in the house when he visited.[166]

It was unlawful for Roman Catholics to hold the advowson whereby Church of England vicars are presented to the parish, but a deed of 1781 shows how Canning circumvented this ruling. Francis Canning leased the advowson to John Baxter, gentleman of Middleton,[167] variously named as Canning's gamekeeper or his steward.[168]

The third and last Francis Canning to be lord of the manor of Ditton Priors inherited the title in 1806. During his tenure the Catholic Emancipation Act was passed giving Roman Catholics the right to stand for Parliament, enter the army and found schools managed by and run for Roman Catholics. No time was wasted, and the school in Middleton Priors was established by 1831, the year of Francis's death. Funding for the school was continued by his widow Jane, who founded a charity for the purpose and for funding a similar school at Illmington near Foxcote. Francis left no heirs, and his brother Robert inherited, but he too had no heirs and lived elsewhere. First Francis and then Robert had taken on the care of their orphaned niece, Eliza Minto Canning, whose father John had died in 1824 when she was 14. When Robert died in 1843, Eliza inherited all the Canning estates of which one small part was the manor of Ditton Priors which brought in an income of £2,735 7s. 9d. per annum.[169]

In the same year that Robert died Eliza married Phillip Henry Howard of Corby Castle in Cumbria. Philip Howard, another ardent Catholic, had taken advantage of the

A drawing of the school in Middleton (SA 3419)

The school building in Middleton as it is today

Catholic Emancipation Act and had become the country's second Catholic Member of Parliament. Ditton Priors was only one of the many manors and lands owned by the Howards who spent most of their time at Foxcote and rarely visited Shropshire. Joseph Bell and his family became the Howards' agents or stewards in the manor. Their story is told in Chapter 13.

CHAPTER 12
The Buildings of Ditton Priors

The oldest building in the parish is the church in the centre of the village of Ditton Priors. As explained in previous chapters, it seems likely that an Anglo-Saxon building predated the present one that dates to Norman times. The south aisle was built in the thirteenth century whilst the spire is of late medieval origin. The trussed rafter roof that spans both nave and south aisle was probably completed in Victorian times and has often been likened to an upturned boat. From the early thirteenth century a church or chapel is known to have existed in Middleton Priors, possibly dedicated to St. Lawrence. We know that it had a belltower in 1318 as an indulgence of 30 days was offered to those who gave money for its upkeep.[170] By this indulgence, the church guaranteed that those who contributed would, after death, spend thirty days less in purgatory before being welcomed into heaven. The chapel also had a graveyard as John Smith in his will dated 1598 stated that he wished to be buried there. The living of the Middleton chapel was linked to that of Deuxhill in the Middle Ages but by 1731 it was again included in the responsibilities of the vicar of

The church c.1900

*The interior of the church c.1890 showing cresting to the screen
that had been removed by 1900 but was recarved by a local carftsman in 2001*

Ditton Priors. It was last used for worship in 1780, and although there is now no trace of it above ground, the name lived on as the field where it was situated was named Lawrence meadow in 1890.[171]

By the mid nineteenth century all the principal farmhouses had been built or rebuilt and in 2004 fourteen of them were subjected to research and dendrochronology.[172] With few exceptions, houses and land belonged to the lord of the manor but it has proved difficult to place tenants in the correct houses before the eighteenth century. Even though the 1728 rental, unlike that of 1768, names the cottagers on Netchwood and Hillside, it does not give the locations of the dwellings, nor does it name the sub-tenants of which there were many. To add to these difficulties, earlier official documents such as rentals, taxations and census returns up to and including 1901, rarely record addresses.

Fifteenth Century

Present day Botwood[173] is a late seventeenth-century house built out of local dhustone, surrounded by a complex of farm buildings. Within the complex stands a cruck-frame barn with a timber felling date of 1477. Evidence within the structure supports the contention that this was once a house[174] and is the only extant building in the parish of Ditton Priors built during the time when the manor belonged to Wenlock Priory. The building of the house coincided with a power struggle at Wenlock when King Edward IV nominated John Stratton for prior, whilst the motherhouse at La Charité nominated John Shrewsbury. The king did not give way in this argument as he had done over a previous

70

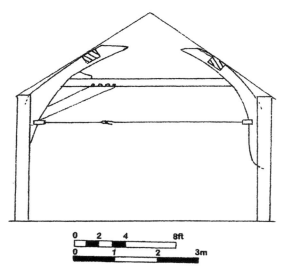

The cruck frame at Botwood reconstructed (with tie-bar) in a drawing by Hugh Bryan

nomination, and John Stratton ruled for eight years. John Shrewsbury was only recognised as prior in 1479, but resigned four years later. Only one more prior nominated by the motherhouse was to rule Wenlock. After 1484, the link with France was broken and in 1494, by an edict from Pope Alexander VI, Wenlock became self-governing with the right to elect its own prior.[175] Such priory politics probably did not overly affect the Ditton Priors population, as by this time most of the principal tenants would have had copyhold leases recorded in the manor courts and would have paid rent to the priory whoever was in charge.

The erection of the cruck-framed barn at Botwood fell half way between two surviving manor court rolls. Each can give an indication of life on the manor. On Tuesday 2 December 1449, the jury sworn in to hear court business are named as: -

William Andrews	Thomas Page	John Page	Radolphus .....
Thomas Andrews	Thomas Grenhull	John Smallman	John Munslow
Gregorie Milward	William Blakeway	Philip Russell	John Coryn

Smallmans, Blakeways and Pages were already an integral part of the manor and their descendants will be found in the new houses of the following centuries. Court business included the case of Thomas of the Downe who brewed ale without a licence, and William Bobyll senior and William Bobyll junior who were given until Christmas to repair their hedges. Thomas Whitwall of Middleton paid 2s. to the lord for the surrender of his lease.[176]

The next court for which we have a record was summoned on 11 November 1510, the jury is named as:

William Smallman	John Page	William Reynoldes	Richard Blakeway
John Markes	Thomas Smallman	Thomas Adams	Roger Scaltoke
William Bulloke	Richard Smallman	Edward Nicolles	Richard Longfield
Edward Catstree			

The tenant of the cruck-framed barn must have been one of the jurors, but his name eludes us. The entries in the court roll indicate the parlous state of medieval housing in Ditton for Thomas Smallman, Thomas Blakeway, John Taylor and Roger Catstree were all placed under an order to repair their houses. Such orders were found in most

71

entries for the next forty years. One other item of interest relates to Middleton mill as a woman, Katherine Haward, tenanted it; she was ordered to mend it before the feast of St. Michael.[177]

Sixteenth Century

In the winter of 1547, only three years after Humphrey Pakington bought the manor of Ditton Priors, timber was felled that soon afterwards became the principal rafters of the building known as **Hyde Farm** in Middleton Priors.[178] The house was built as a box-framed three-bay open hall construction, not too dissimilar to the cruck-framed house of the previous century. An open fire at the west end of the hall was the original method of heating as evidenced by today's smoke blackened roof timbers. Two bays, open to the rafters, were used for social and communal activities, whilst the remaining eastern bay was the service end, functioning as a buttery and pantry. A screens passage separated the two parts. The kitchen may or may not have been detached from the main dwelling, an arrangement designed to prevent a kitchen fire accounting for the whole house.

More is probably known about the owners and tenants of Hyde Farm than any other dwelling in the parish thanks to the foresight of George Smallman, tenant in the 1600s, who left his initials on a door panel. The first tenants are not known, but it seems likely that in the late 1580s Nicholas Smallman, his wife Margaret and their children, who included George born *c.*1590 moved there.[179] The court rolls trace Nicholas's move from Ditton to Middleton about this time, when the smoke bay was removed and chim-

Hyde Farm today, the oldest inhabited house in the parish

Confirmation as to an attested copy of the will of Richard Bartholomew Barnaby Lutley still in Hyde Farm. From this and other documents we were able to reconstruct the ownership and tenancies of the building since Tudor times

Blocked up medieval stairs found during the surveying of Hyde Farm

neystacks inserted. It was probably then that the open hall was also ceiled over and a chequerboard ceiling inserted into the western end room. This ceiling is rather splendid and is similar to one in Wolverton in Eyton-under-Heywood parish that stylistically is dated to the 1570s.[180] The Lutleys, who were known to have owned Hyde Farm in the eighteenth century, had family ties with the Jenks family of Wolverton leading to a supposition that they might have owned Hyde Farm at an earlier date. Like the Lutleys, the Smallmans were ardent Roman Catholics. Nicholas Smallman's son, Samuel, was Humphrey Pakington's priest and there are many nooks and crannies in the building for the hiding of a priest and the chalice, vestments and paten used in the mass if it became necessary. George Smallman lived in this house when his residency certificate was issued in 1628, marking him out as a Roman Catholic. It seems safe to assume that the lord of the manor owned Hyde Farm in 1547, but by 1728, or earlier, the house and lands were owned by Philip Lutley and were in the possession of his son, Richard Bartholomew Barnaby Lutley (who assumed his maternal grandfather's surname of Barnaby) in 1768 when the map and rental were compiled. Richard Bartholomew's son, John Barnaby (who did not use the Lutley surname) sold the estate in 1786 to Hercules Hide whose family owned Ruthall Manor and Oakwood. The Hides sold to the Howard Estate in the 1840s.

A house such as the original Hyde Farm belonged to a medieval

The inserted chequerboard ceiling c.1580 at Hyde Farm

society that required whole families and retainers to be housed under one roof. By the mid sixteenth century, society had begun to change in ways that affected the building and layout of houses. The cash economy increased, tenant farmers paid economic rents and were no longer strictly bound by feudal custom and obligation to the lord. The lords in turn no longer exploited their demesne lands, but came to experience a contractual relationship with tenants. By the mid sixteenth century taxation fell more heavily on the moneyed class than on the landed gentry, consequently money was invested in land and buildings.[181] This sequence of events led to what is generally termed 'the great re-building' when, for the gentry farmers at least, medieval housing stock was replaced by two-storey houses for one family. Ditton clearly participated in the great re-building as many of the larger farmhouses shown on the 1768 map were built between 1570 and 1630.

The most important medieval house in the manor must have stood beside the church for several hundred years before being rebuilt, probably on the site of an older one, in the late 1570s. In earlier times it was probably known as the manor house, but today it is called **Church Farm.** It stands on the 'island site'[182] and in 1580 was timber-framed, but later encased in dhustone. The layout of the house illustrates the transitional stage of sixteenth-century housing, as the eastern end was an open hall, only being ceiled over in the mid seventeenth century whilst the western end was always two-storey with an upper solar.

Door in a first-floor chamber of a house in Neenton showing decoration known as Shropshire swirl

A wall painting, executed about 1600, known as a Shropshire swirl, once graced the solar.[183] Both an inquisition post mortem and a valuation were taken at Humphrey Pakington's death in 1631 when all his goods were listed. Both documents mention a dovecote in the village of Ditton Priors and it seems likely that it stood in the grounds of Church Farm.[184] Dovecotes belonging to lords of the manor were not popular with tenant farmers as the birds ate much of their grain.

Church Farm and its predecessors had always belonged to the lord of the manor, but from the fifteenth century is likely to have housed the many generations of Smallmans who were bailiffs first to the priors and then to subsequent lords of the manor. By 1715, Francis Palmer, originally from Middleton, was the tenant, followed by Francis Reynolds. It is doubtful if Francis Reynolds ever lived in Church Farm, although his son Thomas is listed as his sub-tenant from the 1880s.

Chapel Cottage, so called because it shares ground with the early nineteenth-century Wesleyan chapel, was erected sometime between 1553 and 1585.[185] Initially there were two identical cottages, now restored as one dwelling and

74

encased in local dhustone, but originally timber framed. At the west end are the remains of a croglofft identified from the bevelled edges of the two struts that once formed the entrance.[186] Timbers in the present loft are still lime-washed indicating that the house was once an open hall. Two diagonal fireplaces *c.*1660 can be seen in rooms on the ground

The 1768 map shows the land owned by Thomas Edwards. Below: Chapel Cottage today

floor at each end of the house, whilst a bread oven is associated with the central stack on the ground floor.

The first owner of Chapel Cottage to be identified is T.E. (Thomas) Edwards who appears on the 1768 map. He was married to Ann Hide and their heir, Millonia, married Richard Onslow of Ruthall. Their son, also called Richard, was born in 1771. In 1817 Millonia, then widowed, together with Richard, gifted the leasehold of land next to Chapel Cottage to the non-conformists for the building of their chapel. Millonia died in 1818 aged 73 and her grandson, Thomas, who inherited Chapel Cottage left it to his son Edward. Thomas Edwards and his heirs would not have lived in Chapel Cottage, but tenants cannot be identified until the 1881 census when Richard Aston, carpenter, was in one cottage and William Mansell in the other.

Seventeenth Century

Home Farm at Middleton Priors, with a dendrodate of 1612, is today totally encased in Georgian cladding and attached to the Victorian Middleton Lodge, a three-storied house basically stone-built and roughcast over when the two distinct units were amalgamated. Documentary evidence for Middleton Lodge shows that the edifice was rebuilt in 1761 and again in 1843 when the then lords of the manor used some of its rooms on their rare visits to Ditton Priors.[187] It is thought that Home Farm could have been the service unit of the earlier house. It retains some timber framing internally with lath and plaster infilling

Rear view of Home Farm where it abuts the larger building, Middleton Lodge

and has two large spine-beams with chamfered stepped run-off stops that are typical of the area.

Robert Hassall, father of Thomas at Derrington (see below) was the tenant in 1661 when, in his will of that date, he stated that he held the land by lease from the Right Worshipful Sir Henry Audley. John Miles was tenant in 1716 as recorded in the recusant roll. John came from an old Middleton family whose forebears were millers at Middleton mill in 1544. Arthur Low was the tenant in 1728 and either the same Arthur or his son was there in 1768. The Georgian façade was completed *c.*1771 as in that year Arthur Low took a 21-year lease on '… all that messuage tenement and dwelling house whereof hath lately been erected and built at Middleton including the malthouse'.[188] By 1808 Joseph Edwards tenanted the whole complex with Samuel Reynolds following in the 1830s. The Power family resided there in the 1840s, but their story and that of the next tenant, Joseph Bell, comes in Chapter 13.

Derrington Manor Farm is a recent name given to the largest house in the township of Derrington. The northern end dates from the sixteenth century[189] and was no doubt built during the 'great rebuilding' phase by Humphrey Pakington, lord of the manor. It has a later seventeenth-century stair turret with the original staircase *in situ*. The balusters are in the same style as those of the Hall Farm and date to the last decade of the seventeenth century, suggesting that the same carpenter was used on both houses (see The Hall Farm below).

The earliest residents that can definitely be placed in this house are the Blakeways. Humphrey Blakeway's will of 1632 notes that he is of Derrington and helpfully names his mother, sisters, friends, nephews, nieces and many more. For instance, he writes: 'I give

Derrington Manor Farm today, the home of the Hassall family
in the late seventeenth century

to Florence Jones and Marie Trow, my mother's two maidservants ...'.[190] By the 1680s, Thomas Hassall, his wife Ann and son Thomas were the tenants and it is most likely that the house was modernised in this or the next decade. Ann died in 1688 and was buried in the chancel of Ditton church with an impressive iron grave marker. The Hassalls, as Roman Catholic gentry, were no doubt close to Catherine Barker, the resident lord of the manor who at this time was renovating the Hall Farm. It seems reasonable to conjecture that they shared the same carpenter. In the Recusant Roll of 1715, William Hassall, Thomas's son, listed all his assets and the marriage settlements of himself and his wife.[191]

In 1768, Arthur Low was the principal tenant with 367 acres, and Richard Reynolds followed him in the 1820s.

The timbers in the north-western part of **The Hall Farm** (it is always listed with the definite article) have a dendrodate date of 1627, although it may be that an earlier building is somewhere inside the present one. Catherine Barker, lord of the manor (d.1700) extended the house in 1693 if evidence from an eroded sandstone plaque can be relied on.[192] Catherine's son, Thomas, died in the house in 1704, and his inventory described a layout of the house that has changed little in the intervening centuries. The two self-contained attics, built with reused timber, were for male and female servants. When the house was extended, a partially subterranean dairy was added. Such dairies were typical of the larger farmhouses in the parish. Other features include two wall paintings from the early seventeenth century of different design, 'plank and muntin' doors and 'lambs tongue' stops on the beams.

At least three distinct phases of build can be found in The Hall Farm, the last one being in 1693 by Catherine Barker, lord of the manor

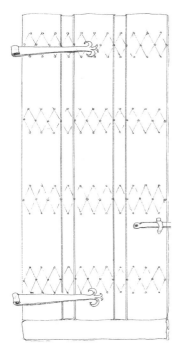

Left: Plank and muntin door found at Hall Farm (drawn by Gill Reilly) Above: The Corner, built c.1620, described by Madge Moran as 'the jewel in [Ditton Priors'] crown'

The Barkers lived in the house until the death of Bestene in 1705 and then it was tenanted as it appears in the Recusant Roll of 1716 as 'The Hall' with John Miles paying £44 per year rental. George Smallman and Lancelot Simkiss appear as tenants after Miles, and in 1808 John Reynolds took on the tenancy and was succeeded by his son Francis, who was the principal tenant of at least three farms in the nineteenth century.

Two more humble dwellings are worth recording here. **The Corner**, in Middleton Priors, a 'squatter cottage', named 'the jewel our crown' by Madge Moran, did not yield a dendrodate, but stylistically dates to the 1620s. It is built of sandstone, most likely from a quarry within a few hundred yards of the cottage. Beams in the downstairs rooms have lamb tongue and pyramid stops and outbuildings include a barn and Victorian privy and pigsty. From the 1890s it has been inhabited by a succession of Garbetts.

Middleton Cottage, inhabited by the Pages in the seventeenth and eighteenth centuries, is charming not least because of its rustic chequerboard ceiling. The cottage is located close to Hyde Farm and no doubt one of the Pages saw the splendid oak ceiling there and fancied one of his own. It is delightful in its own way, but not in the same league as its neighbour down the road.

Eighteenth Century

The cores taken from **The Orchards** provided a very clear date for the felling of the timbers in the spring of 1761. This means that it must have been the newest house in the parish when the estate survey and map were commissioned in 1768. Richard Page was tenant in 1768 with 183 acres whilst his brother Thomas ran Ditton Farm with 468 acres.

The Orchards in the 1920s. Joseph Bell III moved here in the 1920s

Their father, John Page, was tenant of Ditton Farm in 1728 when land of 447 acres was recorded, so Richard's acres did not come at Thomas's expense. The house has the usual subterranean dairy and a 'nearly-detached' kitchen indicating that the risk of fire was feared. Features included a cruck-like apex to the main roof truss and planked fruitwood doors.

1761 was the time when both the yeoman farmers and the first Canning lord of the manor, Francis Canning I, undertook agricultural investment in Ditton. Francis Canning II inherited on the death of his father in 1766 and the estate survey and map were commissioned to ascertain the new lord's assets. Investment continued for another sixty years as New Farm Middleton and Great Leasows are not on the map, but appear in documents dated to the 1820s.

CHAPTER 13
A Manor of the Howards: 1843 – 1920s

One of the first acts of the Howard lordship was the piping of a good water supply from the Brown Clee and other springs into the settlements of Ditton and Middleton Priors. The housing for the Ditton supply, with the monogram PHH and dated 1845, stands in South Road and still gives a steady supply of water. No doubt other notable improvements also took place, new and improved housing for one as there are at least five Howard plaques on houses on the estate. But one issue, a well-documented feud between the Catholics and Protestants of Ditton Priors, dominated the parish documents relating to the 1860s.

Eliza Minto Canning's husband, Philip Henry Howard, was one of the first Catholic Members of Parliament described as: -

> ... a zealous Catholic [who] identified himself with every public movement in further-
> ance of the interests of his religion. His pen was ever ready to defend the rights of the
> body whose cause was nearest to his heart.[193]

Howard's fervour for Catholicism is noted in his support for the Catholic chapel in Middleton Lodge and the Catholic school nearby. In 1851, thirty-six people attended mass in the morning with twenty present at the afternoon service.[194] Monks based at Aldenham Hall, the seat of the Catholic Actons about four miles from Middleton Priors, served the chapel. Most of the worshippers must have been employees or tenants of the estate, as was Michael Power, the steward of the chapel. Power's family tenanted Middleton Lodge/

The water tap in South Road bearing the initials of Philip Henry Howard

Home Farm and he is listed in the 1851 census as both agent of Howard and malster. Some time between 1851 and 1861, Joseph Bell, another Roman Catholic, arrived in Ditton Priors to take over the job of agent. Bell's father, also Joseph, was Howard's steward at Foxcote and Joseph junior eventually moved into Middleton Lodge with his family, whilst Michael Power junior worked with his father taking over the manage-ment of Home Farm by 1871.

Ditton church, which also had a school close by, attracted 67 worshipers to the morning service in 1851, but only 7 in the afternoon. The churchwardens' accounts for the first half of the century show a well-organised parish with musicians playing in the west gallery. These accounts were presented to the yearly vestry meeting held at Easter time, when besides the presentment of accounts, the setting of rates for expenditure on the church, the poor and the highways and the election of churchwardens and other parish officers was undertaken. The meeting, held in the church vestry, was in many ways the successor to the manor courts in its dealing with parochial affairs and the forerunner of the parish council. From 1856 the regular churchwarden accounts of previous years were replaced with irregular, poorly presented ones. Such ill-drafted accounts may have been indicative of the crisis in parish affairs that in the 1860s culminated in county notoriety. One of the sources of the problems is recorded in 1861 by the elderly vicar, Edward Ridsdale, who had served the parish for many years: -

> At a vestry meeting legally called on Good Friday last, and held this Day April 1st 1861, it was resolved that Thomas Goode, Richard Reynolds were chosen church-wardens for the year ensuing – and it was resolved on the motion of Mr. Power of Middleton, seconded by Mr. Joseph Bell that the Church Rate be laid for the ensuing year.

Michael Power Junior and Joseph Bell Junior signed the entry.

So by 1861, two Roman Catholics, who both worked for the Roman Catholic lord of the manor were deeply involved in both Church of England and parish affairs.

The Roman Catholic chapel inside Middleton Lodge photographed in the 1970s.
(Photo: Madge Moran)

Following the death of Reverend Ridsdale, James Butler Wilkinson was instituted as Vicar of Ditton Priors on 21 December 1862. Michael Power junior and Joseph Bell junior continued to sign the yearly report of the vestry meeting. The meeting was chaired by Wilkinson, a formidable man and a vigorous intervener in all parish affairs as detailed in the account he wrote about his years in Ditton Priors.[195] He began his account early in 1863 with a complaint that prior to his arrival a schoolhouse had been erected on glebe land without the necessary conveyance. This school and the accompanying cottage were built on land previously occupied by the medieval vicarage that had been demolished when the new vicarage was built in 1828. Wilkinson believed that this land and the rent thereof belonged to the living and should '... become the special property of successive vicars of Ditton Priors.' Having registered his pecuniary interest in the school through numerous letters to the bishop, he turned his attention to the 'ruinous state of the church'. Meeting with what he said was very little interest in Ditton Priors he sought funds outside the parish and began work on change and restoration. The west gallery was removed, the musicians which Wilkinson recorded at his induction as a choir, double base and fife, were disbanded and probably the medieval plasterwork removed from the internal stones.

Reverend Wilkinson was unable to attend the vestry meeting in April 1867, when Joseph Bell junior was elected vestry clerk, proposed by Joseph Bell senior and Michael Power, senior. As duly elected clerk, Bell took control of the official records of the vestry

Reverend Wilkinson's log book – the choir had a double bass and fife

meetings. Wilkinson was clearly horrified and had no intention of allowing such an appointment as his memo from the minutes of the next hastily called meeting showed: -

> N.B. There was considerable discussion as to whether the office of Vestry Clerk could be held by a 'Roman Catholic' and the vicar as Chairman undertook to bring the matter in question before the Magistrates at the next Quarter Sessions – either for them to confirm or annul the election.

Reverend Wilkinson's record of this meeting on 2 May 1867 in which he referred to himself in the third person, showed something of Wilkinson's manner and how the battle lines were drawn up: -

> The Vicar as Surveyor of Roads proposed a Road Rate of 6d in the pound. Mr. Thomas proposed a Rate of 4d. – the Vicar not deeming the sum sufficient decided to abide by his own judgment in the matter – he as Surveyor having power of himself to lay either one, two or three 10d. rates.

Unfortunately the book that Wilkinson used to record his actions was a joint purchase by the vestry meeting. He wrote: -

> This book having been partly purchased by subscription of 6d, each of several in all amounting to 5/6d and not being considered strictly Parish property the Vicar offered to return 6d. to any party who so subscribed – Mr. Bell senior and Mr. John Thomas received their sixpences – the rest decline to do so.

From now on Wilkinson treated the book as his own journal and records his trials and tribulations with 'the Romanists'. On 7 May he wrote: -

> In consequence of the election of Joseph Bell to the Office of Vestry Clerk … Francis Reynolds and I laid the somewhat informal proceeding before the Magistrates in Petty Sessions.

The matter was reported in the *Bridgnorth Journal* of 11 May 1867. As written, the issue appeared to be about the minute books and not the actual appointment. Reverend Wilkinson pasted the newspaper cutting in his logbook.

A ROMAN CATHOLIC APPOINTED VESTRY CLERK

At the petty sessions on Tuesday week before the Mayor of Wenlock an application was made by the Rev. J.B. Wilkinson of Ditton Priors for the possession of certain books held by Mr Michael Power, a Roman Catholic, whom his brother Romanists and one questionable Churchman had elected by a majority of six to two to the office of vestry clerk. The magistrates ordered the books to be given up. Upon plaintiff asking whether the books should be sent to him, the defendant humorously remarked that plaintiff need not trouble himself; he would bring them up, as it might give him an opportunity of taking a glass of wine with his friend. During the years term of office it is the intention of the incumbent to keep his own books and to render the office as much a sinecure as possible.

The article was incorrect to say that Power was the vestry clerk, Wilkinson was always clear in his log that it was Joseph Bell junior. An editorial in the *Shrewsbury Free Press* ridiculed both the issue and Reverend Wilkinson. His letter in reply explained his reasoning. He said that the Catholics in the parish numbered no more than 35 or 40 against a Protestant population of 615, but he stressed that whilst they may not be numerous, they are 'occupiers of a considerable part of the Howard estate … and the reason why a majority of votes was originally obtained by them can only be accounted for by the … widely prevailing impression that if the others came to vote at the vestry meeting they would be "turned off their farms."'

By now Reverend Wilkinson and the trustees of the Howard estate were in correspondence, the vicar wrote: -

> Will you please let me know whether the tenants of the Estate are at liberty to attend to and vote at all parochial meetings in freedom and without restraint and whether the prevailing impression that if the tenantry come to vote at the Vestry Meeting they will be turned off their farms emanates from the Powers or is merely an idle rumour. I ask this in the interests of 580 souls out of 613.

The reply from Mr. Eyston expressed humiliation at having to answer. assuring the vicar that: -

> the tenantry are perfectly at liberty to vote at all meetings in freedom and there could never be any foundation, in fact for any contrary impression. ... the tenant occupiers have their own interests to protect in the question of Parochial Rates and appointments … I cannot help thinking that the best interest of the Parish will be supplied by a good understanding between the parties & Ratepayers in the Parish.

It is likely that Reverend Wilkinson made known the sentiments of this letter before a hurriedly called vestry meeting on 16 May 1867. Thirty-six people attended (twenty-eight more than the Easter meeting of the previous month) and a resolution to the impasse was sought. A proposal was made that the election of the vestry clerk be declared null and void. Mr Bell and Mr Power proposed otherwise. The first proposal was carried by twenty votes to sixteen. A majority of four does not seem a large number given that this was a parish affair being decided at a vestry meeting held on Church of England premises, although each side must have exhorted their supporters to be at the meeting. In the event, the vicar kept his own minute book for the remainder of the year thus obviating the need for a vestry clerk.

Understanding the nuances of being a Howard tenant or depending on Michael Power or Joseph Bell for estate work is difficult to assess at this remove, but it may well be that the smaller tenants did fear for their livelihoods and both Michael Power and Joseph Bell lived in the parish whereas Howard and his trustees did not.

Well before the Easter vestry meeting of 1867, Reverend Wilkinson circulated a printed letter to all parishioners. It concluded: -

> As your truest friend, I shall for the future most carefully watch the progress of Parish affairs, and on your behalf demand that they be strictly conducted according to Law – justice and equity being extended to each and all alike. For the future, then, by your independent votes, place those only in positions of trust who will devotedly study your best interests, and advance the well-being of the Parish, and let the so unfortunate past be buried in oblivion.

The 1868 vestry meeting did not quite go as the Reverend Wilkinson hoped. The matter of the vestry clerk was resolved, but despite proposing himself, the vicar failed to be elected Surveyor of Roads and called for a ballot to be held the following month. This involved a lot of organisation and ballot boxes at strategic points around the parish. The teller of the votes was Joseph Bell who announced that the vicar had lost the ballot. Reverend Wilkinson refused to accept the result. No poor law rate and no highway rate were set for that year.

The vicar's log does not make it clear how, or indeed if, the matter was resolved. By the summer of 1868 the consuming passion recorded in his logbook was the founding and training of the village cricket team. An uneasy truce appeared to have been declared as Michael Power was the team captain and by 1870 he is recorded as chairman of the vestry

*Middleton Lodge c.1900. Joseph Bell junior (Wilkinson's vestry clerk)
is on the extreme right (Photo: Shropshire Archives)*

meeting. Reverend Wilkinson's tirades against both Bell and Power became heated again in 1873 when they opposed his argument that as the National Board School in Ditton Priors was built on church land, it should be transferred to the control of the Church of England. No mention was made in the log of the Catholic school in Middleton Priors, one and a half miles away, but it was probably an incentive for the zealous clergyman to want church control over the other school in the parish. Wilkinson was successful in this campaign. The complaints in the logbook cease in 1876 when Philip Henry Howard died. The log continued with other parish matters including the distribution of money, bread and coals to the recipients of the Barker Charity until Wilkinson died on 27 July 1886.

In the nineteenth century, four non-conformist chapels were built in the parish. The Wesleyans met in Ditton Priors in 1801, or maybe earlier, and by 1816 had built their own chapel with seating for 120 people in Chapel Lane, now a private house. In the same year, the Primitive Methodist chapel on Hillside was built which in 1851 claimed an afternoon attendance of 60 to 80 worshippers. Both Lower and Upper Netchwood also had Methodist congregations in the mid-nineteenth century when they met in residents' houses, the chapels being built later in the century.[196] It may be that attendance at such places of worship was boosted by the ill feeling that must have been generated by the feud described above.

The Break-up and Sale of the Manor of Ditton Priors

An agricultural recession was underway when Eliza and Philip Howard's son, John Philip Canning Howard, inherited the manor in 1876. The price of cereals had collapsed due to bad weather and to the increasing quantity of cheap grain from North America, Australia and New Zealand.[197] The Howard estate was not faring well. In 1878 Derrington Farm was 'in hand', namely run by the estate and not a tenant, and several rents were in arrears.[198] John Howard had inherited all the Canning estates of his mother and with his own holdings in Cumbria he probably decided it was time to retrench and the whole manor of Ditton Priors was placed on the market in 1878. Catalogues and maps were produced, but no buyer came forward. In 1879, another attempt was made to sell part of the manor. Joseph Bell, Howard's Agent wrote: -

> The Ditton portion of the estate was offered for sale by auction on 26 July last at Shrewsbury, firstly in one lot and afterwards in twelve lots, but no acceptable offer was received for any portion of it.[199]

Rent reductions were made during the early 1880s when many tenants received a remission of up to 15%. In 1882, Viscount Boyne of Burwarton Hall bought *c.*1,050 acres in Ditton Priors and at the end of the decade another 745 acres. By 1890 the Boyne estate, consisting principally of Ditton, Powkesmore and Hillside, was being run as a separate entity from the Howard estate of Middleton Priors, Middleton Baggot, Lower and Upper Netchwood and Lightwood.[200] Lord Boyne had bought land containing Brown Clee Hill but the twentieth-century story of the exploitation of its mineral wealth belongs in the next chapter.

In 1919 all Lord Boyne's lands in Ditton Priors were offered for sale when many sitting tenants bought their holdings. William Lowe, publican and farmer, bought the Howard Arms with 68 acres of land for £3,850. Many small tenants also bought their cottages. Sam Hall, a quarryman, then living at number 2 Middleton Road (now Station Road) paid £100 for his semi-detached sandstone 'villa' with pigsty and half an acre of land built in 1890 by the Boyne estate.[201] Sam Hall made his mark on the conveyance beside the flourished signature of Frederick Gustavus Hamilton-Russell, Lord Boyne's brother and agent.

'Squire' (John Philip Canning) Howard and his wife Alice in c.1915

In the 1920s many of the farms and houses on the Howard estate were also offered for sale and again sitting tenants, such as the Corfields at North Farm and John Childs at Derrington bought their holdings.

The 1920s also saw the demise of the manorial system and in 1925 copyhold tenure was finally abolished. By the time of John Howard's death in 1934, being lord of the manor was an honorary title only, but one that his only child, Lady Ursula Lawson, took seriously as inhabitants of Middleton Priors remember her interest in the Catholic chapel and school. In the 1930s the last of the Howard lands were sold and the lordship of the manor appears to have slipped into abeyance.

CHAPTER 14
Industry on Brown Clee

Geology of the Clee Hills
A simple description of the geology of the Clee Hills will explain why their mineral deposits have been the focus of industry over the centuries. In the Silurian period, (*c*.435-405 million years ago) the area was a vast inland tropical sea whose floor was initially built up from the sands washed into the water. During the Devonian period (*c*.405-355 million years ago) mountain building uplifted the sea floor and only occasionally in the arid climate were non-marine sands and limestones derived from freshwater lakes, able to settle. One of these cleaner limestones, containing the remains of freshwater fish became the commercially viable Abdon limestone beds. In the Carboniferous period (*c*.355- 290 million years ago) seas invaded the eroded mountains, only to be gradually forced back by vast deltas and swamps, in which lush vegetation, such as tree ferns, decayed and were taken into the earth to become first peat and then the coal seams of the Clee Hills. Due to these stagnant conditions and the inundations that occurred, iron was deposited in the shales between the coal seams. During the late Carboniferous period the earth's inner molten rock, or lava, began to ooze through fissures in the sandstone, limestone, and coal measures laid down in earlier periods. This lava soon cooled and consolidated into

A geological model of the Brown Clee hill (Andrew Cobb)

The deed of c.1260 by which Walter Clifford of Corfham
granted a licence for the digging of coal in the Forest of Clee

basalt, known locally as dhustone. At one time there was a large landmass of such mineral measures, but over millennia it was worn away by succeeding eons of glaciation, rain, and frost, but the dhustone covering the caps of the hills gave protection to the mineral deposits below and the Clee Hills were born.[202]

The Early Years of Mineral Extraction – Stone and Coal

Previous chapters have shown that dhustone had been quarried on the Clee Hills for thousands of years. Bronze Age and Iron Age peoples as well as the Norman builders of the twelfth-century church used it. The twelfth- or thirteenth-century nave of the present church must have been built in the lordship of Hugh de Perriers (1155-1175) or an early Prior of Wenlock (see Chapter 6) who gave permission to quarry the stone, and it is possible that one or both of these lords also gave licences to dig for coal although no record of such extraction is found. The first documentary evidence of an owner of the Brown Clee exploiting its mineral wealth relates to Walter Clifford of Corfham, lord of the Forest of Clee. Around 1260, Clifford granted a licence to 'dig coal within the Forest of Clee, or to sell it or to give it away'.[203]

It seems likely that the extraction of stone and its associated coal continued for the next few hundred years, but it is only in the mid seventeenth century that Ditton Priors got its first mention of a collier when Thomas Sherwood was recorded as such in the taxation records of the 1660s.[204] In 1697 Thomas Garbett, collier, of Ditton Priors and Richard Brazier, yeoman, of Cleobury North bound themselves to Robert Cresset for the sum of £60. Details of the bond make it clear that Richard Brazier was the 'sleeping partner' and that Thomas Garbett was the man responsible for repayment of the money, more than likely using it to purchase equipment and a licence to dig for coal. Garbett and Brazier signed the agreement with 'T' and 'R'.[205] Colliers such as Sherwood and Garbett may have dug shallow bell pits or other surface workings but also sank deep pits where they abstracted the coal from an area of the seam before considering it more economical and safer to move along the seam and start afresh.

This Thomas Garbett may have been the man who married Elizabeth Botfield of Abdon in 1676. or perhaps more likely, his son Thomas, born 1677, and therefore 21 at the time the bond was signed.[206] Thomas's brother, John Garbett, born in 1679, tenanted Powkesmore Farm until to his death in 1728 but as this farm had only 47 acres of land, it seems probable that both brothers engaged in digging for coal, possibly in the surface workings or coal pits whose remains can still be seen on the hill above Powkesmore. It is not only male Garbetts who enter the archives at this period. The constable's report for the year 1672 states, 'I present Elizabeth the wife of Thomas Garbett for making a blood and affray upon Thomas Evans'.[207]

At the time of Archdeacon Plymley's visitation in 1794, seven colliers were resident in Ditton Priors out of a population of 608.[208] Sometimes charcoal burners were known as wood colliers, but it seems likely that Plymley recorded coal diggers. Maybe some of the colliers recorded by Plymley worked for Thomas Blount who had paid £20 to Francis Canning for the lease of the coal works in 1781,[209] and although 'Blunt and Bache' were listed in a rent book of 1816 as renting a colliery, it is unlikely to be the same man and may even be a different colliery.[210] One of Plymley's colliers may have been Eusebius Cooper, who was 'killed by the damp of the coal pit' and buried on 29 August 1818.[211]

The 1841 census shows eight miners, all living on Hillside. Three direct descendants of Thomas Garbett, who in 1697 bound himself to Robert Cressett for the sum of £60 to begin coal mining, were amongst their number: another Thomas, together with Richard and John Garbett.

Thomas Garbett and Richard Brazier bind themselves to Richard Cresset for the sum of £60 in 1697
(SA 5460/8/4/2)

Iron Mining (see map p.*xii* for location of furnaces)

Iron working was known in Shropshire from early times. The raw materials were to hand, ironstone itself is found in most of the Shropshire coal measures alongside the limestone that acts as a flux. Coppiced woodland, the raw material of charcoal, and the fast flowing streams of Shropshire provided the power. The furnace at Bouldon was operating in the 1640s when 63 tons of ordnance was sent via Bridgnorth to support the king's cause in the Civil War. A similar amount was made in 1644, including a gun to defend Ludlow. The furnace took its fuel of cordwood from Ditton Priors and its ironstone from Brown Clee.[212] Cordwood is a measure of wood which in 1616 was recorded as 8ft x 4ft x4ft. (This was the standard Midland measure for cord for the seventeenth and eighteenth centuries and indeed probably for long before and after those periods.) The wood was turned into charcoal, probably close to where it was coppiced, before being sent to the furnace. The amount of charcoal and ironstone needed indicates the large volume of traffic that must have travelled on the road that went over Brown Clee to Cockshutford past Nordy Bank and on to Bouldon.

The furnace at Norncott in the parish of Abdon was also in operation about this time and Sir Humphrey Briggs of Ernestry and Abdon no doubt sent his ironstone and limestone there whilst it was in operation.[213] He leased his part of Brown Clee for iron mine production in January 1690/91 charging 15s. for the licence to dig and 2s. for every dozen strikes of iron extracted.[214] In a similar deed dated 1734, Sir Humphrey's interests are made clear: whilst the licensees, the Tasker brothers, can dig for coal and iron, Sir Humphrey has 'free liberty … to hunt, hawk, fish and fowl upon the said premises'.[215] In 1712 'A Mapp of the wasts of the Mannor of Ernestry from the top of the Clee Hill to the inclosures' surveyed for Sir Humphrey mark a spot just below the rampart of the hillfort called 'Davises' Hole' which may be a coal pit.[216]

Charlcotte, the other furnace in the locality, had a local connection in that the lord of the manor of Ditton Priors and her family had a proprietary interest in the venture. In 1678, Mary Yate, the eldest daughter of Humphrey Pakington, lord of the manor of Ditton Priors (d.1631) owned the part of the manor where the furnace was located, although the deed does not state whether there was an operational furnace there at the time. An operational furnace is recorded in 1712 when the registered owners were Mary Audley (Mary Yate's niece who owned a half share in the manor of Ditton Priors) and Mary Yate's daughter, Appollonia. In 1712, Mary Audley and Appollonia Yate sold the land of Charlcotte and the furnace to Richard Knight of Bringewood near Ludlow where there was another iron furnace.[217] If a furnace at Charlcotte was in existence earlier than 1712, it seems likely that cordwood, charcoal, ironstone and coal from the manor of Ditton Priors went to Charlcotte during this time, but once the Knight partnership owned the furnace, the trade from the Brown Clee to Charlcotte became more commercialised.

The Knights expanded the business in the 1720s and 30s by leasing the right to take ironstone from Brown Clee from some of the many owners of the district to whom they then paid royalties. Brown Clee landowners in receipt of such royalties included Francis Canning of Ditton Priors, Bernard Holland of Burwarton and William Poyner of Ludlow. Once the royalties were paid, the abstraction of ironstone and its associated limestone was the business of the Knight partnership who already owned the stone and coal of Titterstone. The Knights do not appear interested in Brown Clee coal as they probably had enough for their business from Titterstone Hill.[218]

The estate survey of 1728 showed that Francis Canning, lord of the manor of Ditton Priors, was making plans to profit from the iron mines on Brown Clee and the local furnaces.[219] The survey listed both coal and iron mines on the hill although no value was placed on them, probably because he had already sold the iron rights to the Knight partnership. The survey recorded many acres of established or planned coppices no doubt intended for the local furnaces: altogether the acreage intended for coppices amounted to nearly 300 acres, 6% of his total estate.

When Francis Canning II inherited the manor of Ditton Priors in 1766, mineral extraction in the Ditton Priors portion of Brown Clee was mechanised. The 1768 map that accompanies the survey shows a gin pit, namely a horse-operated winding device for lifting, and a building with a chimney. The building may have been a stable and smithy, as blacksmithing skills would have been much in demand in the extraction business.

Large-scale iron working on Brown Clee came to an end in the 1790s when Charlcotte and Bouldon had closed, although it seems likely that some mining continued as other local furnaces were still in existence.

Lime Working

In the eighteenth century quarrying limestone around the Brown Clee must have been in full production along with the ironstone mining, but Plymley recorded just one 'limeman' in 1794. In August 1809 the coroner reported that Benjamin Massey of Ditton Priors had died through being suffocated in a quarry, which at this date was probably for limestone. Another coroner's report in 1834 is more specific when Thomas Sherwood's death is recorded as due to a fall of limestone in the quarry.[220]

In 1810 two enterprising brothers began the process of leasing the lime works and a colliery on Hillside from Francis Canning. The negotiations were not without difficulty as George Albot, Canning's agent, wrote to the solicitor to defer the making of the lease: -

> The brothers William and Richard have disagreed with each other so that William Hall says that he will not have anything to do with the works … I believe that William Hall is the aggressor and that Richard in case he could find another partner that would be approved of by Mr Canning much wishes to have nothing to do with his brother … but will, if permitted, take the lease without him.[221]

The rift was healed, as for the next six years William and Richard Hall ran the lime works, but there must have been underlying tension because on 10 September 1816 Henry Fellows signed an article of agreement to become William's partner. The agreement made it clear that Francis Canning owned the limekiln and that Hall and Fellows were just the lessees. Numerous accounts show that in the 1820s William Hall delivered coal and lime, usually at 10s. per load, to every farmer and business in Ditton Priors. The business prospered as Hall and Fellows appear in the 1831 rental paying rent for their coal and lime works of £45 per year. Many loads went to Francis Canning's brick kiln at Powkesmore that was fully operational in the 1820s. One document, dated 1827, showed that the lime house on hillside was built prior to this date. On 6 May 1827 George Morris took on the tenancy of a cottage on hillside and a piece of land described as 'above the lime house'.[222]

Some time after 1841 a windmill was built on Hillside for in the census of 1851 William Evans, a 'Lime Mine labourer', is shown as occupying it.[223] The windmill was built for grinding corn, but because of its position away from the prevailing wind it was never successful, although it did provide a dwelling house for a succession of lime workers.[224]

Ten years later, lime working on the Brown Clee was in serious decline and although James Bowen of Hillside was recorded as a limeman in Ditton Priors, the 1861 census returns from Cleobury North state that their decline in population was attributed to the closing of the lime works.[225] For the next forty years the limekiln at Ditton continued to operate as in each succeeding census, until 1901, one limeman or lime burner is recorded.

It is difficult to find evidence for dhustone quarrying on an industrial scale on Brown Clee in Victorian times, although quarrying the stone was underway from the 1860s on Titterstone.[226] Dhustone was much in demand for both road surfacing and for tram setts, and it seems likely that Brown Clee stone was also quarried for use on the roads. In 1901 some stone extraction was underway, as for the first time one 'dhustone quarryman', Joseph Bradshaw, is listed in the census – but it was a labour intensive industry with the stone coming down hill on horseback or even on the backs of men and women. All was to change as the quarries on both Brown Clee and Titterstone Clee began to gear up for a more mechanised production.

Twentieth-century Dhustone Quarrying

When the 8th Viscount Boyne bought the Ditton Priors half of the manor in 1882, he already had coalmining interests in his native County Durham and must have considered the potential for a more commercial quarry on Brown Clee. By 1900 Lord Boyne with other entrepreneurs had joined forces to develop a dhustone quarry on Brown Clee whose product would travel by incline railway into Ditton Priors and then by light railway to the Great Western station at Cleobury Mortimer. The Cleobury Mortimer and Ditton Priors Light Railway Order was granted on 21 April 1901, a board of directors was formed and negotiations began with contractors to build the railway which would run 12 miles 1 furlong and 7 chains 'or thereabouts' between these two centres.[227]

Engineers' reports were produced to encourage investment. Mr Auden of Bewdley

The 8th Viscount Boyne.
(Photo: Viscount Boyne)

94

This photograph, taken somewhere on Hillside, of Dr Hodges dates to the 1880s. His immunisation kit is strapped to his saddle. Dr Hodges was the first of three doctors of that name to serve the Brown Clee parishes

reported that the dhustone of Brown Clee was of a better quality than that of Titterstone, as it would not become so quickly polished and slippery when used to surface a road. Mr Auden had obviously been briefed to cover all eventualities. His report also stated that several old coal shafts could be re-opened to provide the boiler fuel and the workmen's cottages should remain the absolute property of the quarry company, as 'men will think twice before striking and giving trouble when notice to quit them will be given to them as a consequence'.[228] Such reports were intended to convince the Great Western Railway that it would be wise to invest in such a well organised business, but after many months of prevarication, the GWR declined to become full working partners and the Board were forced to fall back on their own resources.

Smith and Beddoes (1980) detail the many more delays to the work and, only in 1906, when Bott and Stennett put their money and expertise into the venture, did construction work start. In January 1907 men came from near and far to construct the railway, some of them living in two navvies' huts at the

The incline in 1932

95

Ditton Priors end of the incline. Thomas Henry James, aged 47, who lived at Mount Flirt in Neenton was one of the early labourers. He started work as a general labourer digging out the cutting for the incline. On 5 April 1907 an embankment collapsed onto Thomas causing internal injuries. Despite Dr Hodges arriving within 15 minutes of the accident, Thomas died an hour later. Information from the family says that his wife, Eliza, was baking bread when she heard the news and travelled to the scene in a horse and cart, still with her apron on and her hands covered in flour. Nellie their youngest daughter was just three years old.

Despite such tragedies, work on the incline and the light railway continued apace and the opening of the freight service began on 19 July 1908. Unfortunately, Viscount Boyne had died in December 1907 and did not see the official opening.

The drumhead at the top of the incline when in use (at 18 feet diameter and 20 feet wide then the largest in England), and the base in ruins today (Photo: Hugh Bryan)

The Abdon Clee Stone Quarry Company

Naturally, the company was intended to open as soon as the incline was completed, but because of the delays, it was not fully operational until 1908. From its inception to its demise thirty-seven years later, its managing director was James Cross, always known as Hamish.

A quarryman's life was hard and disciplined. The 10-hour day's work began at 6am, which for many meant rising much earlier in order to make the walk from home to the top of the hill. Some of the men were day labourers and even after the walk were not guaranteed work. Before 1914 most of the stone was used for tram setts and men would work in the open chipping the stone into 6 by 9 inch setts. After the war, the length of the working

Quarrymen in the early 1920s

day was reduced by 2 hours and work began at 7am. Until 1918, horses were used to move the stone from the quarry faces to the crushing machinery. A locomotive would then transfer the processed material in trucks to the top of the incline where the largest drum-head in the country controlled the descent into Ditton Priors. After 1918, ex-war department locomotives, known as 'whizz-bangs' were used and horses were relegated to a subsidiary role.[229] Horses were still used on occasions after 1918 as the clothes of the quarrymen in the undated photo above seem to belong to the 1920s.[230] Ditton Priors villagers tell how their ancestors traipsed up the hill calling at one of several shops on

Hillside stores where bread and baccy were sold

Hall Farm Road in the 1920s

Hillside for tobacco and bread, worked all day in the quarry, came home to eat and then tended their gardens or allotments until dark. Many of them lived to a good age.

Hamish Cross in the grounds of Oldfield built from the pre-cast concrete that he pioneered. (Photo: Michael Birt)

Before the First World War the innovative Abdon Clee Stone Quarry Company built houses in Hall Farm Road for their expanding workforce. The date of the build is not known, but Ditton Priors parish registers recorded the first baptism of a child from Hall Farm Road in December 1913.

In these pre-war years, the company established a small tarmac plant at the top of the hill where tar was mixed with dhustone chippings to make 'Asphalt Carpet'. Products made with tar were so successful that a further tar plant situated behind the railway station in the village of Ditton Priors was created a few years later. Towards the end of the war Hamish Cross was instrumental in setting up the pre-cast concrete works. It was a proud boast that anything could be constructed of the resulting concrete panels and posts and to prove it, Hamish Cross had a house built for himself and his family at Oldfield in Ditton Priors.[231]

After the war, five smallholders' houses in Ditton Priors, each with several acres of land, were built for 'returning heroes' complete with barns, privies and pigsties, all from pre-cast concrete. Concrete fence posts and steps seen today on

Brown Clee are a measure of the ingenuity of Hamish Cross's concrete works. These innovations were intended to compensate for the decline in tram setts during the 1920s, although the need for track ballast increased and with the new products the quarry company continued to prosper.

In the late 1920s and early 1930s, when the country was suffering a general depression, more than 200 people were employed in the many aspects of the dhustone business. Although men came in search of casual work, local men predominated on the pay roll. The roll call of quarrymen included many

The locomotive, Trent, *working the quarry in the 1920s*

Cartwrights, Morrises, Hodnetts and Halls, although new surnames and new occupations appear in parish records at this time. Reg Green, who may be related to earlier Ditton resi-

Ruins at the quarry today. (Photo: Hugh Bryan)

The ruins of the crushing house at the quarry. (Photo: Hugh Bryan)

dents of that name, was the explosives man in the quarry. He lived at 1 Hall Farm Road, and it was his daughter Eva whose baptism was recorded in 1913.

In the 1930s the dhustone cap had all but disappeared, and the company began to dig ever deeper in search of dhustone. The large crater opened up by this process became known as the Crane Hole or sometimes Lake Kilowatt. By 1937, the dhustone was worked out and the quarry ceased operating. When the Light Railway order was granted in 1901 the height of Brown Clee was recorded as 1,792 feet or c. 545 metres.[232] By the time the quarrying finished in the 1930s so much dhustone had been removed that the height of Abdon Burf had been reduced to its present height of 540 metres.

CHAPTER 15
The Twentieth Century

The demise of the Saxon manor of Ditton Priors and the successful growth of industry, detailed in previous chapters is only part of the story of the late nineteenth and twentieth century Ditton Priors. Other aspects of social and economic events and the people involved give a more complete picture of life in the parish.

Ditton Priors Brass Band
Churchwardens' accounts show that as early as 1827, a band that included a viol and flute played at church services and would have been based in the west gallery. The accounts

South Road, Ditton Priors c.1907, taken from a magic lantern side held by Rowley House Museum, Shrewbury

Ditton Priors Brass Band in the 1890s

detailed repairs to the west gallery stairs in 1850. No trace of the gallery can be seen today, so we can no longer 'turn and face the music' as the saying goes. The Reverend Wilkinson wrote in his logbook in 1863 that the church band consisted of a choir, a double bass and a fife and the whole ensemble was conducted by John and Thomas Hodnett. John Hodnett had led a village band as early as 1858 as the *Bridgnorth Journal* reported their playing in September of that year at the celebrations of the marriage of the Hon. Gustavus Hamilton Russell to the Lady Katherine Scott. The Hodnett brothers, originally from Neenton, are recorded in the 1871 census as tailors, although by this date it would appear that Reverend Wilkinson had installed an organ, thus rendering the church band redundant. Music making was clearly important to the Hodnetts and other members of the band, as by 1870 the Ditton Priors Brass Band was an important part of village life.[233] Maybe by this date they also had their splendid uniforms, no doubt made by the Hodnett brothers. The band was paid £4 to play during a three day church bazaar held in August 1887 to raise money for a 'Falkirk' stove for the church. Church accounts showed that the money was paid, but the weather was so bad that the tent in which they were to play blew down.

The band was very popular and much in demand for social functions in the wider area as illustrated by one of the weekly letters that the land agent, Joseph Bell, wrote to the lord of the manor, John Philip Canning Howard. Bell wrote that in June 1897, Ditton Priors had celebrated Victoria's golden jubilee with a very fine queen's procession, but

The band in the 1920s and Alfred Morris, one of its last bandmasters

that the rest of the rejoicing had to be postponed until the following day, as he had been unable to obtain the services of the band, 'they having engaged themselves to go to Stanton Lacy'.[234]

When John Hodnett died aged 60 in 1880 the leadership of the band passed to his brother Thomas. Thomas was deeply involved in parish affairs, he rang the church bells and when he died in 1908 aged 77, he had been the parish clerk for 36 years. Both Alfred Morris, born in 1867, and his cousin Tom Morris, born in 1877, became bandmasters after the death of William Hodnett. At this time Tom lived at Woodend and had mastered the trombone and many other instruments including the organ that he played at Bent Lane chapel for over 40 years. He died in 1968 aged 91.

The band was a family affair. Will, Thomas Hodnett's nephew also played and several generations of the Morris, Cartwright and Bowen families, most of whom worked for the Abdon Clee Stone Quarry Company, constituted the majority of players throughout the years of the band's existence. In the twentieth century, band practice took place on Hillside, either in a barn or in the lime shed. After practice members would adjourn to 10 Hillside, the home of bandsman William Morris, 'to quench their thirst'. Jim Parker, grandson of William Morris, told stories of men staggering home across the fields by the light of hurricane lamps after such refreshments.

The *Wolverhampton Journal* recorded one of the last engagements of the band in

1919. Ditton Priors' war dead numbered twenty, but the whole village rejoiced when peace was declared: -

> The managing director (Mr. Hamish Cross) of the Abdon Clee Stone Quarry Co. and the employees of the firm decided to hold the Peace celebrations on Monday. They invited the parishioners of Ditton Priors to join them ... A substantial tea was provided for all parishioners and the Ditton Priors Brass Band kindly gave their services. Dancing was enjoyed by a large number of people in the evening, and at the close there was a display of fireworks.

For reasons that are not clear the band was disbanded in the 1920s, and the instruments sold. The drum, however, remained in the house of William Morris to be banged each evening by his grandchildren, Jim and Sheila Parker.

Jim Parker with the band's drum

The Parish Council

The vestry meeting had been the organisation for parish affairs since Tudor times, but the Local Government Act of 1894 specified that in parishes of more than 300 inhabitants a parish council should be elected. In December 1894, under the chairmanship of Thomas Bell, a parish meeting was held at which nine Ditton Priors councillors were duly elected. Although Joseph Bell, Howard's land agent and Reverend Wilkinson's erstwhile opponent, took the chair at the first meeting, rivals were proposed and officially George Green was the designated chairman in the first year. Joseph Bell did not allow this situation to continue and from the start of the second year, he took the chair that he maintained until his death in the early 1920s. His son, another Joseph, living at The Orchards, took on the chairmanship in 1931 and held it until June 1940 when an entry in the minute book reads: -

> It was proposed by F. Smallman and seconded by H. Bowen that owing to his internment as Treasurer to the Fascist Party Mr. Bell's name be removed from the Council. (Carried)

Ditton Priors Railway station in 1907 (Photo: W. Atkinson)

Other parish councillors were not so contentious although there are a few references to demanded resignations from those not considered to be doing their duty. The first female councillor, Mrs. Emily Jane Lowe, appears in 1934, and it can be assumed that she was elected following the death of her husband, Councillor Ernest Mainwaring Lowe.

From 1900 to 1906, the parish council continued to support the Cleobury Mortimer and Ditton Priors Light Railway and when the venture finally got underway in 1907, the councillors felt justified in their action: -

> To take a little whiskey to mark the commencement and drink to the success of the
> Ditton Priors and Cleobury Mortimer Light Railway.

Despite its proper title, whenever the name of the railway is recorded, Ditton Priors takes precedence over Cleobury Mortimer. Such approval did not stop subsequent councillors from engaging with the managers from time to time about blocked footpaths and dilapidated stiles on railway land.

Hardly a meeting goes by without a mention of complaints from parishioners about the poor state of the highways and byways of the parish. Concern about increasing traffic on the poorly maintained roads is noted in 1949 when councillors expressed concern about 'the speed of the traffic through Ditton Priors'.

Education and self-help were much in evidence in the first two decades of the twentieth century and the parish council took advantage of many courses on offer. In 1908 lectures on soft cheese making were given, followed by home nursing and care of stock. From 1914 lectures took place in the reading room in Chapel Lane, funded by the Hon. Eustace Scott Hamilton-Russell, Arthur Bott and William Stennett, managers of the quarry and railway company.

The parish council noted problems with public wells, particularly one in Netchwood that they considered dangerous and from 1919 they maintained the three water fountains in the village. Following a survey of villagers in the 1940s a limited supply of electricity was brought into the village area only. Hillside, Bent Lane and Powkesmore had to wait

No electricity yet – Number One Bent Lane in the 1920s. The home of Martha Pritchard (pictured)

until the 1950s before they were included in the supply.

Only occasionally did national affairs or matters of wider importance than the parish of Ditton Priors get mentioned. In the minutes for 1914-1918, not one word pertaining to the war was made and even during the 1939-1945 war, when five Ditton Priors' men were killed, only the issue of gas masks and the raising of funds for the returning troops gave an indication that anything out of the ordinary was occurring.

Ditton Priors did not miss out on national celebrations. Victoria's jubilee was celebrated (although the band may have been a day late) as were subsequent coronations and jubilees. Almost the last entry in the minute book described the eight months of preparation and planning that preceded the 1953 coronation.

Ditton Priors Schools

From the eighteenth century there is evidence of a school in the village of Ditton Priors. In 1719 pupils had to attend church and learn the catechism and in 1794 a schoolmaster and two or three women teachers were recorded.[235] In 1821 a new school was built which took girls as well as boys, and Reverend Wilkinson's logbook recorded that prior to 1862 a school had been built on glebe land besides the church. It is this building, with various modifications, that became the board school of 1871 with Church of England control granted in 1876. The Roman Catholic school built and subsidised by the lords of the manor in Middleton Priors must also be remembered, but it is the registers of the Church of England school in Ditton Priors that allow anther glimpse into early twentieth-century Ditton Priors history.

The registers from 1876 to 1914 recorded 62 Cartwrights, 45 Morrises, 22 Evanses, 19 Corfields, 17 Childs, 12 Reynoldses, 11 Lowes, 9 Coopers, 9 Smallmans and 4 Hodnetts. Reynolds and Smallmans were surnames found in the parish in the fifteenth

Benjamin Morris, wheelwright, c.1900, one of the many Morrises mentioned in the school records

century, but many of the other common names are also of long standing. Any mention of twentieth-century surnames must include the record in the 1901 census of Richard Smallman, aged 19, whose occupation is given as blacksmith. This entry comes 472 years after the first Richard Smallman is recorded in Ditton Priors in 1418.

In 1901, the registers recorded occupations such as gamekeepers, hoop shavers, shoe-makers, drainers and of course innumerable labourers. These workers and their families constituted a population of only 505, the lowest number recorded since official records began in 1801. By 1911, the registers showed quarrymen, railway workers and other associated trades that contributed to a population of 619, rising to 650 ten years later. From the details on 'father or guardian' in the school registers it is clear that some children are recorded as having a guardian who was not their real father. For instance, Samuel Hall, quarryman, was shown as the guardian of several children who did not share his surname. It seems likely that Sam and his wife may have been early foster parents and looking after 'parish children'.

In the 1880s and 1890s children were leaving school at the age of 10 or 11, but at the turn of the century the school leaving age was nearer 12. Only by 1914 were children staying on until the age of 14. From 1908 to the 1940s less than ten boys and no girls were transferred to grammar schools, proving just how difficult it was for bright boys to get a further education and almost impossible for girls.

The admissions book for the Second World War shows evacuees arriving in Ditton Priors as early as 1939, with the last few coming in 1944. Most came from Liverpool or Wallasey, but home towns were recorded as far afield as Bristol, Birmingham, Wolverhampton and London.

The Royal Naval Armaments Depot: 1940 – 1965

By 1939, the government began searching for storage sites for the vast quantities of armaments that were being produced. Ditton Priors proved to be an ideal site as it was located in the countryside and had good rail access. The quarry had closed a few years before, but the concrete plant was still working, as was the tar plant by the station, although both had closed by 1942. The Cleobury Mortimer and Ditton Priors Railway still carried freight but had closed to passengers on 24 September 1938. A square mile of land besides the station was compulsorily purchased from landowners, the principal of whom was Lord Boyne, and work began building a large complex of buildings and roads. By 1941, the Royal Naval Armaments Depot, Ditton Priors was opened for business. The work produced by the building and the staffing of the depot gave work to local men recently made redundant by the quarry business and to men and women for miles around. For many years more than 30 buses a day ferried workers into what the workers called the 'arms dump' or just 'the dump'.

The depot was of strategic importance and several searchlight batteries and decoys were situated in the hills around to deceive enemy aircraft. Smith and Beddoes report that Ditton Priors was important enough to be mentioned by Lord Haw Haw on the German wartime radio broadcasts.[236] Heavily laden ammunition trains came into the depot almost continuously, but apart from a German plane crash on Brown Clee Hill and a few bombs

Depot Office staff in the 1940s

dropped near Cleobury Mortimer, Ditton Priors, the line and the depot came through the war unscathed.

Ditton Priors had an active Royal Observer Corps, set up in 1939, when their head-quarters was just a tent on what is now the playing field. Soon a wooden hut with a stove and bunk beds and a raised platform, known as the pulpit, was erected and the watch for enemy aircraft continued 24 hours a day seven days a week until 1945. Local men were the watchers, including Doug Morris and Harry Hurskine who was in the habit of walking to the Howard Arms with an old enamel jug and returning with a few pints to help pass the night away. When Coventry was bombed the conflagration was seen from Ditton Priors.

When the war ended the Naval Depot continued to operate and so did the Royal Observer Corps. In 1961, the R.O.C.'s hut was demolished and an underground room approximately 4 metres by 3 metres and some 2 to 3 metres below ground was constructed. Ventilation shafts were the only objects that could be seen above ground. The room was fitted with bunks, a pump and shower for those unfortunates who, it was presumed, would have to read the Ground Zero Indicator above ground after a nuclear bomb had burst.[237] By the late 1970s, Bill Lowe, who had been active in the unit since 1949, and John Hinton were responsible for training the other eight or so volunteers, but with the ending of the Cold War the group disbanded.

Although the passenger train service had closed in 1938 on Good Friday, 1965, a special train carrying many railway enthusiasts steamed along the Ditton Priors to Cleobury Mortimer line to mark the final closing of the railway. The end of the Royal Naval Depot came in the same year although its demise must have been in sight for some-time as a thorough survey by the Admiralty in 1958[238] can only have been undertaken with

The last passenger train from Ditton Priors 1938 (Photo: R.K. Cope)

a view to sale and dispersal of the assets. In the summer of 1966 the Ministry of Defence began negotiations with the previous owners of the land, who under existing legal precedents were entitled to buy back their land at the original price paid by the government. Lord Boyne began his negotiations for the return of his land and also expressed interest in buying another 140 acres at Ditton Priors. Negotiations were well advanced with the District Valuer and a date of 17 January 1967 had been made for the parties to agree a final figure for sale. Unknown to the section within the Ministry of Defence that was negotiating with Lord Boyne and other local landowners, another section of the same ministry had given permission for Ditton Priors to be a base for the U.S. Army, part of N.A.T.O., who had been given short notice to quit France. A letter, dated 1 February 1967 to the Prime Minister from Patrick Neane, Minister of Defence, made it clear that the Minister of Defence (Administration), Mr. G.W. Reynolds had 'publicly apologised for the inconvenience caused to Lord Boyne in the House, on BBC TV, Midlands Local News Service and by a personal visit to Lord Boyne at his home in Shropshire'.[239] But Lord Boyne and the other landowners had to wait for the return of their land. Indeed a few elements of the U.S. Army had arrived a few weeks before when the *Bridgnorth Journal* reported that an 'advance guard' of 200 men with huge military vehicles rumbled through Bridgnorth on their way to their new quarters.

The Americans in Ditton Priors
The 233 men of the 608th Ordnance Company, of the U.S. Army arrived in January 1967, but by April only a few remained. Their main task had been to prepare the base in order to store 22,000 tons of ammunition that had to be moved from their French base. Once this

was done and the ammunition stored, the majority of the soldiers left for their base at Fort Benning in Georgia, leaving only a few personnel and civilian staff. At this time, the First Sergeant Lawrence Patchen wrote to the *Bridgnorth Journal*: -

> As first sergeant in charge of the company and a professional soldier, my tours of duty have taken me round the world, and it has been very refreshing and enjoyable to know that people from two different countries can meet on a common ground without the friction and strife that seems to dominate the world today.. So from the bottom of our hearts we, the N.C.O.s and men of 608 Company want to say Thank You.[240]

The remaining American soldiers stayed in Ditton Priors for only another fifteen months, but it is remembered as a time of great excitement. About 100 local people found work on the site, including Cecil Bradley, who worked as a security man on the base. The soldiers went out of their way to woo the local people, opening their social clubs to villagers and organising many shows and fetes to entertain the locals. It was with much regret that, in June 1968, the Americans departed and Cecil Bradley lowered the flag for the last time.

As the American Army leaves Ditton Priors and the land is finally, if a little late, returned to its previous owners or new owners, it is time to leave the history of the parish. From now on the history of Ditton Priors is within living memory

Cecil Bradley helps to lower the flag as the Americans leave Ditton Priors in June 1968

Bibliography

Abbreviations used

BL	British Library
HRO	Hereford Record Office
NA	National Archives
NLW	National Library of Wales
SBT	Shakespeare Birthplace Trust
SA	Shropshire Archives
TSAS	Transactions of Shriopshire Archaeological Society
TWNFC	Transactions of the Woolhope Naturalists' Field Club
VCH	Victoria County History
WCRO	Warwickshire County Record Office
WRO	Worcestershire Record Office

Bailey, Mark *The English Manor* Manchester Universality Press, 2002

Bassett, Steven *The Origins of Anglo Saxon Kingdoms* Leicester University Press, 1989

Blair, John *The Church in Anglo-Saxon Society*, Oxford University Press, 2005

Brown, Mary Gifford *An Illuminated Chronical,* Bath University Press, 1990

Bryan, Hugh *From Psalms to Souza: The Story of Ditton Priors Brass Band*, 2004

Chibnall, M. *The World of Orderic Vitalis* Boydell Press, 1984

Dansbury, Don *The Lady Who Fought the Vikings* Imogen Press, 1993

Dyer, James *Hillforts of England and Wales* Shire Books, 1992

Edwards, A.J.M. 'An Early Twelfth Century Account of the Translation of St. Milburga of Much Wenlock' in *TSAS* Vol. LVII, 1961-1964

Eyton, Rev. R.W. *Antiquities of Shropshire*, Beddoe, 1860

Finberg, H.P.R. *The Early charters of the West Midlands* Leicester University Press, 1972

Foster L. & Alcock L. (eds.) *Culture & Environment*, Routledge & Keegan Paul, 1963

Gelling, Margaret *Signposts to the Past* Dent & Sons, 1978

Gelling, Margaret *The Place -Names of Shropshire*, Place name Society, 2001

Gelling, Margaret *The West Midlands in the Early Middle Ages* Leicester University Press, 1992

Grandsten, Antonia *Historical Writing in England 550-1307* Routledge & Keegan Paul, 1974

Hillaby, J. 'The Origins of the Diocese of Hereford' in *TWNFC* Vol 42, 1976

Hinton, John *Wheathill* Orphans Press (no date)

Hinton, John, *ABC of Three Villages* Orphans Press (no date)

Hodgetts, Michael *Life at Harvington 1250-2000* Archive of Birmingham Historical Commission, 2002

Hodgetts, Michael 'The Origins of Recusancy:The Pakingtons 1530-80' in *Midland Catholic History* No 4, 1995

Hodgetts, Michael 'The Yates of Harvington' Reprinted from *Recusant History,* 1995

Hooke, D. *The Droitwich Salt Industry an examination of the West Midland Charter Evidence* in British Archaeological Reports No. 92 (1981)

Hooke, Della & Burnell, *Simon Landscape and Settlement in Britian AD 400-1066*, University of Exeter Press,1995

Hopkinson, Beatrice Salt and the Domesday Salinae at Droitwich A.D. 674 to 1690 Droitwich Brine Springs & Archaeological Trust with the Worcestershire Archaeological Society, 1994

Hoskins,W.G. *Local History in England*, 1972

Jenkins, A.E. *Titterstone Clee Hills* A.E. Jenkins 1983

Laflin, Susan 'The Ford Place-Names of Shropshire', MA Thesis, 2000

Malpas, A.; Butler, J.; Davis, A.; Davis, S.; Malpas, T.; Sanson, C. *The Early Church in Herefordshire*, Leominster History Study Group, 2001

Mercer, Eric *English Architecture to 1900: The Shropshire Experience* Logaston Press, 2003

Millett, Martin *The Romanisation of Britian* Cambridge University Press, 1990

Moran, Madge *Vernacular Buildings of Shropshire* Logaston Press, 2003

Morgan, Philip *Domesday Book and the Local Historian* The Historical Association, 1988

Morris, Richard *Churches in the Landscape*, Phoenix Grant, 1981

Mumford, W.F. *Wenlock in the Middle Ages* Mumford, 1977

Pretty, Kate 'Defining the Magonsaete' in Bassett, 1989

Ranford, R.J. 'The History of Ditton Priors', paper given to Bridgnorth & District Historical Society 1936

Rowley, T. 'The Clee Forest – A Study in Common Rights' in *TSAS* Vol. LVIII, 1965

Smith, W. & Beddoes, K. *The Cleobury Mortimer & Ditton Priors Light Railway* Oxford Publishing Company, 1980

Stamper, Paul *The Farmer Feeds Us All* Shropshire Books, 1989

Stanford, S.C. *The Archaeology of The Welsh Marches* Collins & Sons & Co., 1980

Stenton, Frank *Anglo-Saxon England* Oxford University Press, 1971

Tinder, Barry *A History of Shropshire* Phillimore, 1983

Toghill, Peter *Geology in Shropshire* Swanhill, 1990

Victoria County History Volume X Oxford University Press, 1998

Webster, Graham *The Cornovii* Duckworth, 1979

Webster, L. & Webster, V. 'The Pakingtons of Harvington' in *Recusant History* Vol 12 No 5 April, 1974

White, Roger & Barker, Philip *Wroxeter - Life and Death of a Roman City* Tempus Books, 1999

References

1. Stamper (1989) p.1
2. Shropshire Sites & Monuments PRN 04113
3. Shropshire Sites & Monuments PRN 02725, however the Chitty papers in Shropshire Archives throw doubt on the find saying that it may have been exchanged with another
4. Shropshire Sites & Monuments PRN 03758 found 1982
5. Shropshire Sites & Monuments PRN 02817
6. Shropshire Sites & Monuments PRN 03214
7. Shropshire Sites & Monuments PRN 02600
8. Chitty L. *The Clun-Clee Ridgeway – A Prehistoric Trackway across South Shropshire* in Foster and Alcock (Eds.) (1963) pp.171-176
9. Shropshire Sites & Monuments PRN SA 04112
10. SA 365/41 Lily Chitty Collection
11. *VCH* Vol I p.329
12. SA Lily Chitty Collection 365/36
13. Dyer J. (2003) p.29
14. Stanford (1980) p.90
15. Ian Richman *The Cornovii* in Foster and Alcock (Eds.) (1963) p.251
16. Webster (1975) p.20
17. *Ibid*
18. I am grateful for information from Dr Andy Fear, lecturer in Ancient History at Manchester University who says that this is known to have happened in the Spanish Roman provinces
19. White & Barker (1999)
20. A decree of Emperor Constantine ordered all Roman towns and cities to have a Christian church. Archaeological excavations are ongoing at Wroxeter
21. Richman, Ian '*The Cornovii*' in Alcock & Forster (1963) p.251
22. Identified at Stoke on Trent Pottery Museum
23. Mercian Day School 28 January 2006 led by Dr. Steven Bassett, Head of the University of Birmingham Department of Medieval History
24. For more detailed information see Finberg (1972) and many others
25. Finberg (1972) p.217 quoting Goscelin
26. Pretty in Bassett (1989) p.175
27. *Ibid*
28. Morris, R. (1989) p.100 says that many early monasteries were on sites of Roman villas and some Roman archaeology has been found in the grounds of Wenlock Priory
29. Finberg (1972) pp.147-148
30. *Ibid*
31. Hillaby (2001) in Malpas, Butler, Davis & Davis p.41
32. I am grateful for information from Dr. Margaret Gelling, which identifies the name 'Clee' found in such place-names as the Cleoburys, Clee Stanton, Clee Downton etc. as belonging to one estate. Dr. Gelling also suggests that the Rea valley may have been another estate or sub-estate in that the place-name 'Neen' is found in Neenton, Neen Savage, Neen Sollars etc
33. Stenton (1971) says that villages or nucleated settlements as we know them today did not become a feature of the landscape until at least the tenth century.
34. Archaeological evidence from Tamworth and Winchcombe shows that defensive ditches and ramparts were in place before the defences constructed in the 10th century by Aethelflaeda and Ethelred. (Mercian Day School)
35. Savage, Anne (1982) *The Anglo-Saxon Chronicles* Macmillan p.93
36. Gelling (1992)
37. All these names can be found in the four volumes *The Place-Names of Shropshire* by Dr. Margaret Gelling, English Place-Names Society
38. Dr. Margaret Gelling is convinced that this derivation of Doda is correct, however she does cover the possibility that the name may mean a rounded hill top

39. SA 6000/6948-7001 land charters that give details of these place-names and many more
40. Bassett, Steven (1966) *The Administrative landscape of the diocese of Worcester in the tenth century* in Brooks & Cubitt (eds) *St Oswald of Worcester – Life and Influences* pp.147-173
41. Finberg (Ed.) *The Agrarian History of England and Wales* 43-1042 (1967) p.422
42. Mercian Day School
43. Finberg (1972) p.148
44. Finberg (1972) p.90
45. I am indebted to Dr. Charles Kingsley, an Anglo-Saxon specialist, from the University of Christchurch etc. for this theory
46. Hopkinson (1994) p.15
47. Caynham was heavily wooded and Donington was part of the forest of Brewood in pre-conquest times. Clearly these were areas where hunting took place
48. Rowley (1965) p.48
49. Morris, R. (1981) p.212
50. Dean Plymley's visitation in the 1820s records the building of the new vicarage. The site of the vicarage is blank in 1768 as the map only depicts manorial possessions
51. Eyton (1860) identifies only Ashfield and Middleton, but says Sidnall, Derrington, Powkesmore and Hudwick should constitute the remainder. However there is no evidence that Powkesmore was ever a township
52. Morgan (1988) quotes Sally Harvey who suggests that the ploughland figures represent a new fiscal contemporary with Domesday itself and indeed part of its purpose, p.21
53. Morgan (1988) p.23
54. Morgan (1988) p.22
55. Hopkinson, 1994 p.31
56. Mumford (1977) pp.11-12 the prior is so called because he owes allegiance and money to the mother-house whilst an Abbot owes allegiance to the diocesan bishop
57. Grandsten (1974) writes that Goscelin was a conscientious researcher and both Finberg and Gelling rely on his sources
58. *Testament of St. Mildburh* in Finberg (1972) p.197
59. Mumford (1977) p.15
60. Chibnall (1984) p.26
61. Eyton (1860) Vol 3 p.330
62. Recorded in the Pipe Rolls for Henry II
63. Eyton (1860) Vol. 3 p.346
64. Information from the *Inspectimus* (Patent 22 Edward III p. 3 m. 34) as detailed in Eyton (1860)
65. Eyton believes this charter to have been written when the King was at Bridgnorth in 1177 Vol. 3 pp.264-264
66. Eyton is here quoting from a charter written in Normandy in 1170
67. Eyton
68. Rowley (1965) ignores Eyton's theory stating that he believes the Royal Forest of Clee was attached to Corfham in Saxon times, but for reasons discussed in the previous chapters this does not seem to agree with known facts and Eyton's theory that it was attached to Ditton seems more likely
69. A 'haye' is a small hunting park where the deer and other game such as wild boar are completely enclosed within a pale or hedge. The significance here is that the king's writ does not hold sway as it does in a royal forest
70. Rowley (1965) p.48
71. Eyton (1860) 'The Clee Forest Vol 5 p.197
72. *Ibid*
73. Shropshire Feet of Fines A.D.1218-1248 pp.391-2
74. SA 6000/6952 John of More or John the Woodward, Wenlock's first recorded forester lived at Middleton Priors
75. Inspeximus (Pat.22 Edward III p. 3 m.34) This document names Nicholas as vicar, although no mention is made of whom or what institution has the rectory

76. Inspeximus Episcopal Acta Hereford – Hugh Foliot 1079-1234 p.288
77. Derived from the Latin *itinere* meaning journey
78. Shropshire Eyre 1256, Seldon Society, 1981, Crown Pleas p.240
79. Mumford (1977) pp.66-67
80. Entry fines relate to the money paid by tenants in order to take on a lease. This may be when a lease is inherited or when the Lord found new tenants
81. Entry Fines SA 1037 no. 26
82. Inquisition Nonarum 1341
83. SA 1224/2/1 1344-1345
84. Quoted in Stamper (1989) *The Farmer Feeds Us All*
85. SA 5112/2/2 and 1224/Box 342
86. Mumford (1977) pp.25-26
87. SA 6000/6974
88. SA6000/6978
89. *VCH* Vol X p.311
90. BL Add. Ms. 6164
91. SA 1224/2/6
92. Farming the land for the benefit of the Lord of the Manor
93. Borough of Much Wenlock 1468-1969 Corporation Minute Book
94. SA 5112/2/5
95. See Chapter 9
96. E 303/14/247
97. Deed of Surrender quoted in Mumford, (1977) p.81
98. Letters Patent SA 422/1
99. *Ibid*
100. *Ibid*
101. Some of the original plaster can still be seen after a Victorian 'makeover'
102. Inventories of Church Goods, Shropshire Temporalites of Edward VI TSAS Vol. XII p.93
103. Manor Court Roll 7 July 1550
104. First Chapter Act Book HRO
105. P.C.C. Wills F30 Ketchyn
106. Inventory states 9 March 1578/0
107. Humphrey always signed his name 'Humfrey', but I will use the conventional spelling to ensure continuity
108. Hodgetts (1995) p.1
109. A process by which the estates of convicted recusants was leased to a third person with profits going to the Exchequer
110. Webster & Webster (1974) p.207
111. Acts of Privy Council 1595-96 as quoted in *VCH Worcestershire* Vol 3 pp.50-51
112. Hodgetts (2002) says that the priests' holes have all the trade marks of the great hide builder Nicholas Owen
113. Webster & Webster (1974) p.207
114. Such names appear as church wardens and in connection with Ditton church
115. To be found in Warwick County Record Office CRO 1379/1-20 and Hereford Record Office T74/359
116. Information from Introduction to Ditton Priors Manor Court Rolls 1510 – 1614 by Dr. Sylvia Watts
117. Frankpledge dates back to Anglo-Saxon times when each tithing, or ten households, were held jointly responsible for their good behaviour. In the sixteenth century it was a mechanism for regulating the administration of the various villages and hamlets that comprised the manor of Ditton Prior
118. At various times Deuxhill and Pickthorn also make presentation at the manor court of Ditton Priors even though they are some distance away
119. Rowley (1965)
120. The one addressed to Ditton is transcribed in SA 5112/4/2/1
121. Wills and Inventories in Hereford Diocesan Records and Family Record Centre, London

122. Tarver, Anne (1995) Church Court Records p.1
123. Transcribed by Christopher Potter in HRO
124. Dendrodating reveals timber-felling dates in the last thirty years of Humphrey Pakington III. For example Home Farm in Middleton has a felling date of 1612
125. Mercer (2003) p.136
126. The date the timber was felled
127. See Chapter 12 for more details of the houses of Ditton Priors
128. NA E/179/167/200
129. The 1728 estate survey – see Chapter 11 – shows newly enclosed fields
130. All from Hereford Record Office, a list of goods taken on death
131. This John Taylor is the churchwarden whose name is carved along with that of John Smallman on a church pew. The carving is dated 1666
132. As quoted in *VCH* Vol X p.311
133. Near Tenbury Wells
134. Hodgetts notes in *The Yates of Harvington* p.150 that Sir Henry professed to have conformed *c*.1640, but this appeared to make no difference to his fines and the sequestrations of his property
135. Calendar for the Committee for the Advance of Money (29 June 1644)
136. WRO 899:115/2
137. *VCH Worcestershire* Vol 3 pp.50-53
138. Living in the house now known as Hyde Farm
139. Roman Catholic Certificates of Residence TSAS 4th Series Vol.X p.270
140. Francis Ellis cannot be traced in any other record of Ditton Priors
141. Multiplier suggested by W.G. Hoskins (1972) *Local History in England* pp.172-173
142. Religious Census 1676 in TSAS Series 2 Vol 1 pp.75-91
143. SA Q/1/Box 1
144. The Yopps are named as Anabaptists in another parish record
145. SA Q1/1/Box 1. It is not known why the bridge is named thus, although this appears to be the land leased by Thomas Plowden in the fourteenth century
146. SA Q1/1/Box 1
147. SA The Hearth Tax Roll of 1672
148. Recusant Roll SA QE/3/3/1
149. Sold by Canning in 1730 to Lord Wenlock of the Monkhopton Estate. *VCH* Vol X p.317
150. 735/6 Details of interest on loans paid by Canning to Mr. Colebatch and Francis Hassall
151. Stamper (1989) p.49
152. SA 6000/487
153. In the 1720s Botwood and Hyde Farm belonged to Barnaby Lutley's father Philip who married Penelope Barnaby. Their son took his maternal grandfather's name when he inherited his Worcestershire estate. Both Hide Farm and Botwood were sold by John Barnaby, Barnaby Lutley's son, in 1786
154. By which he means that the commons and wastes which were still available to the cottagers for grazing
155. SA 6001/6864
156. Dodd, J. Phillip (1954-1956) 'The State of Agriculture in Shropshire 1775-1825' in *TSAS* Vol LV 1954-1956 – Dodd does not show where this quote comes from
157. SA 3419 Box 3
158. SA Q1/8/38(2)
159. Barker Charity Book in the possession of Ditton church
160. Poor Law Abstract HC 82 pp376-377 (1818) xix as quoted in *VCH* p.315
161. NA MH12 9850
162. Family history information from Pauline Kilford of Telford reveals that Margaret was most likely to be the Margaret (then known as Cartwright, the surname of her last foster carers) who married Edward Wyre in 1876 and one of her direct ancestors
163. Copy of Act and accounts in SA 3419 Box 2
164. *VCH* Vol X p.312
165. The Abstract of Title for Middleton Lodge shows that Anthomy Kinnersley had owned it in 1684 when

it was occupied by John Miles, ploughwright It was sold to Richard Smallman and then to Thomas Hassall in 1691

166. SA 3703/14
167. WRO CR1379/Box 4 The deed mentions both the vicarage of Ditton church and the chapel at Middleton Bagot that was still in existence at this time
168. *Shropshire Journal* 17.9.1794
169. Cumbria Record Office D/HC1/31
170. A method whereby a core of timber is taken and dated by comparison to core samples from a database
171. Reg. T. de Cobham as quoted in *VCH* Vol X p.318
172. Information from *VCH* Vol X p.318
173. Called Botwood because people of that name owned it in the 19th century. The present house dates to 1681-92
174. Identification made by Madge Moran, Shropshire's leading architectural historian of timber-framed buildings
175. Mumford (1977) p.31
176. SA 1224/2/1d
177. WRO CRO 1379/1-20
178. First named as such in 1841 when Thomas Hide owned it
179. George is reported in the manor court of 1602 as having failed to swear allegiance to the queen, an act usually performed by boys of 12
180. Moran (2003) p.67
181. Mercer (2003) p.136
182. See Chapters 4 & 5
183. Identified by Catherine Baird, Conservation Officer, North Shropshire in 2002. Churchyard Farm in Neenton also has a Shropshire swirl, so called because they appear to be unique to this part of the country
184. SBT DR/5/1397
185. No exact date could be ascertained from dendrochronology
186. A Welsh word denoting a sleeping chamber under the eaves accessed by a ladder
187. SA 6000/728
188. *Ibid*
189. It was not possible to get a dendrodate from Derrington manor, Dating is from VCH and Madge Moran
190. Will in HRO
191. QE/ 3/3/1
192. Ranford (1936) noted the plaque on the Hall Farm stated CB 1693 – indecipherable today
193. Gillow Vol.3 p.442 as quoted in 'Catholic Members of Parliament 1829-1885' by John A. Stack in *Recusant History* Vol. 24 No. 3 May 1999 p.388
194. 1851 Religious Census
195. Wilkinson Log in possession of the church of Ditton Priors
196. *VCH* Vol X p.319
197. Stamper (1989) p.60
198. *VCH* Vol X p.312
199. SA 3419 Box 5, Book 7
200. *VCH* Vol X p.312
201. Annotated copy of sale catalogue in possession of Ditton Priors Local History Group
202. Peter Toghill (1990)
203. NLW Castle Hill 2633. Like most thirteenth-century deeds, it is not dated. The National Library of Wales catalogue it as first half of the thirteenth century, but Rowley (1965) states it to be *c*.1260. There is evidence that Walter de Clifford was lord of Corfham in the 1250s. He died in 1266.
204. NA E/179/168/214
205. SA 5460/8/4/2
206. No definite link can be made with the later Botfields, ironmasters of Coalbrookdale, although their family tree acknowledges the Abdon Botfields

207. SA Q1/1/Box 1
208. SA 6001/6864
209. 6000/735
210. WRO CR 3419
211. Parish Records
212. *VCH* Vol X p.150
213. *VCH* p.398 - Norncott
214. A strike is a measure of ironstone and a dozen strikes is estimated to be in the region of 36 to 40cwt. Arthur Raistrick *Dynasty of the Iron Founders* (1989) William Sessions Book Trust pp.36 & 37
215. SA 5735/2/2/4
216. SA 1037/
217. SA 757/62/1 & 2
218. WRO 10470/4,5
219. SA 6000/734
220. SA Q1/1 Box 1
221. SA 3419 Box 2 all details in this section are from this box of accounts
222. SA4149 Box 3
223. The plot of land containing the windmill, built of limestone, is described in the Enclosure Act of 1841 and no mention of the windmill is made
224. W. Seaby & A. Smith *Windmills in Salop* Stevenage Museum 10 18. I am grateful to David Poyner and Tim Booth who both visited the windmill to discuss its purpose and to Paul Brennan, the owner, for access to the site
225. *VCH* Vol II p.232
226. Jenkins, Alf (1983)
227. This section draws heavily on Smith and Beddoes (1980), the definitive work on the Cleobury Mortimer and Ditton Priors Railway and its associated dhustone quarry
228. As quoted in Smith & Beddoes p.12
229. Smith & Beddoes p.75
230. I am grateful to the family of Alfred Morris for this previously unpublished photograph
231. Now Oldfield Nursing Home
232. *VCH* Vol I 1908
233. Information from Mrs Ruby Ford quoted in Bryan (2004)
234. Cumbria Record Office JAC/7/60
235. *VCH* Vol X p.319
236. Smith & Beddoes (1980) p.85
237. Information from Bill Lowe
238. Author's Collection
239. NA PREM 13/1593
240. Information and letter from *Bridgnorth Journal* dated 21 April 1967

Index

Also from Logaston Press

The Folklore of Shropshire
by Roy Palmer

Shropshire's folklore is presented in a series of themed chapters that encompass landscape, buildings, beliefs, work, seasons, people, music and drama. In the eleven chapters the county's rich store of folklore unfolds in a way that allows you to dip into what most intrigues, or to read from start to finish. Here are stories of mark stones, stone circles, giants, tunnels, dragons, rivers, meres, pools, hills, church sites changed by the devil, vengeful spirits, bull and bear baiting, cockfighting, fairs, herbal remedies and those which involve peculiar activities, minstrels, histriones, waits, charmers and 'cunning folk', ghosts, witches, bountiful cows, of characters such as the early saints, Caratacus, Edric the Wild, Humphrey Kynaston, Jack Mytton and even recent folklore surrounding Hilda Murrell, of tales of the Civil War and of Hopton Quarter, of celebrations and customs surrounding times such as Easter, Christmas, All Souls' Eve, Ascension Day and Palm Sunday along with the likes of 'burning the mawkin', 'tin panning' and wife selling, of rhymes that link villages, ballads that tell of events in the county's past, of folk plays and mummers—to mention just some of what is included.

ISBN 1 904396 16 X (978 1 904396 16 1)
Paperback, 320 pages, over 250 illustrations   Price £12.95

The Churches of Shropshire & their Treasures
by John Leonard

This book explores 320 parish churches of Shropshire, half of them medieval. Chapters guide the reader through changing architectural styles, from Anglo-Saxon origins to the 21st century and then detail the treasures of the churches, including towers and spires, porches roofs, sculpture, fonts, memorials and monuments, stained glass, rood-screens, pulpits, pews and chancel furnishings. The county is then divided into geographical areas, with descriptions of all the individual churches in each area.

John Leonard is a retired consultant physician who lives in Shropshire and has written numerous books on churches.

ISBN 1 904396 19 4 (978 1 904396 19 2)
336 pages, over 530 illustrations   Price £12.95

Also from Logaston Press

Some Shropshire Gardens Revisited
by Barbara & Alan Palmer

Written and researched by two dedicated plant and garden lovers, the book describes 50 gardens scattered across Shropshire, most of which are open to the public at various times during the year. The book is crammed with information, observation and pictures that includes: the history and development of each garden; what there is to see; unusual plants and trees; practical advice on the care of plants; ideas for garden design and planting tips. Alan and Barbara Palmer have lived in Shropshire most of their lives making and nurturing three gardens, all of which are open under the National Gardens Scheme.

ISBN: 1 904396 34 8 (978 1 904396 34 5)
Paperback, 128 pages 130 colour photographs   Price £9.95

Cinderallas & Packhorses:
A History of the Shropshire Magistracy
Edited by David J. Cox *and* Barry S. Godfrey

This book provides a very readable and clear picture as to how the early forerunners of Justices of the Peace came about during the reigns of Richard I, Edward I and Edward II, and developed over time. The duties that Justices of the Peace have had to perform have been varied and encompass collecting rates for the repair of bridges, trying those accused of felony and trespass, the regulation of wages and prices, the maintenance of gaols and Houses of Correction, the suppression of disorderly houses, appointment of parish constables, tracing and prosecuting recusants, controlling of riots, fining women deemed to be living idly, judging those killing game, licensing of alehouses, dealing with vagrancy, administration of Poor relief, ensuring the maintenance of a bastard child by its alleged father, ordering people to the stocks or whipping post, dealing with those who uttered a profane oath, judging those who worked on a Sunday, administration of the county rate, the regulation of Turnpike Trusts, supervising the administration of asylums, the formation of police forces and, most recently, dealing with many motoring offences — and that is not a definitive list. These and other duties are all covered. The book successfully explains what was happening nationally, as well as the concerns, issues, and some of the cases that were being dealt with locally. It ends by raising the issues that face the Magistracy today, not least in terms of the professionalisation of the service, and the tension between use of local knowledge and a desire by central government for blanket uniformity.

ISBN: 1 904396 45 3 (978 1 904396 45 1)
Paperback, 112 pages, 30 illustrations   Price £9.95